Christian hope encom[passes the day when] suffering will be no m[ore ...] sin—which Christ bore for us—will be no more (...; Isa. 53:4; Gal. 3:13), for "the first things have passed away" (Rev. 21:4). This day is coming but is not yet here; it is the day we long for when we will know the fullness of salvation in Christ. Until that day, sin, suffering, and sickness are both a part of a groaning creation (Rom. 8:19–25) and a means through which God works His sanctifying grace, molding us into the image of Christ (Rom. 5:1–5; James 1:2–4).

Joe Whiting has written a book, *Viewing Sickness Biblically*, that helps us to embrace God's will in sickness and to grow in faith and love for Christ. It is a book that gives us hope and encourages us to see the goodness of God and the wonder of grace more fully through suffering, as well as help with the specifics of how to get to there. *Viewing Sickness Biblically* is a book written by one who has tasted the kindness of God in Jesus, lived the truths and principles he writes about, and set an example, in his own life, of following Christ, for us to walk behind (1 Cor. 11:1).

- Joey Newton, Pastor of Newtown Bible Church, Newtown, CT; MDiv, The Master's Seminary; PhD, Southern Seminary

The current culture seems to think that you have to have experience with an issue before you can even speak about the issue. If you share that perspective, this book is for you because Joe Whiting has experienced suffering. But more important than Joe's experience with suffering is Joe's theology of suffering drawn directly from Scripture. There is great benefit in being taught by someone who has suffered. There is greater benefit being taught by someone who believes in the inerrancy and sufficiency of Scripture to help those who suffer.

- Bud Moss, Pastor, MDiv, The Master's Seminary, Pine Grove Baptist Church, Leesville, SC

Viewing
SICKNESS
Biblically

Viewing
SICKNESS
Biblically

How to Make
SENSE *of Seemingly*
SENSELESS *Sickness*

JOSEPH WHITING

FREE GRACE PRESS

Viewing Sickness Biblically

Copyright © 2021 by Joseph Whiting

All rights reserved. Written permission must be secured from the author to use or reproduce any part of this book, except for brief quotations in critical review or articles.

Unless otherwise indicated, Scripture taken from the New American Standard Bible®, Copyright © 1960, 1971, 1977, 1995, 2020 by The Lockman Foundation. All rights reserved.

Published by Free Grace Press
1076 Harkrider
Conway, AR 72032

freegracepress.com

Cover Design by Scott Schaller
Typesetting by InkSmith Editorial Services

ISBN: 978-1-952599-35-4

Contents

Introduction: Everyone Gets Sick 1
1. Categories of Causality 5
   The Curse for Sin 5
   The Results of Sin 7
2. Aspects of Causality 9
   Punishment or Chastening 9
   Repentance 11
   Natural Consequences 18
   Wrong Thinking 25
3. Why Beneficial Sickness Might Sound Odd 51
   Because We Might Not Be Biblically Minded 52
   Because Our Theology Might Be Wrong 55
   Because We Might Have the Wrong Focus 57
4. Six Benefits of Sickness 61
   God's Glory 61
   Christlikeness 72
   Realism 78
   Hope 84
   Comfort 94
   Ministry 100
5. Conclusion 111

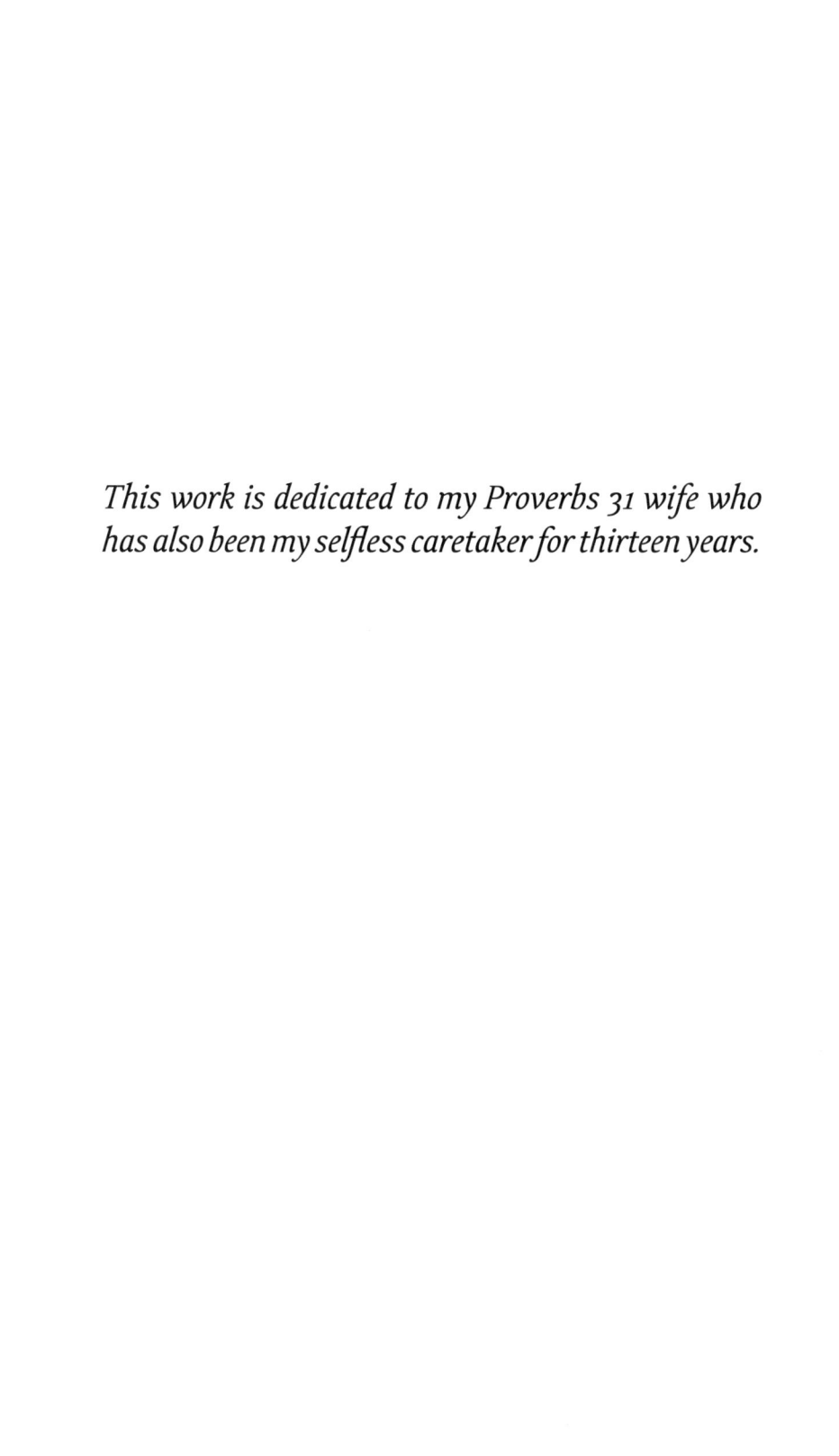

This work is dedicated to my Proverbs 31 wife who has also been my selfless caretaker for thirteen years.

Acknowledgments

Special thanks to Dr. Robert Smith MD, whose book *The Christian Counselor's Medical Desk Reference* had a large impact on my thinking about and structure of this work.

Introduction

Everyone Gets Sick

Everyone gets sick. Every person in the history of the planet has dealt with sickness to one degree or another. All people on the planet must experience sickness. Thus, the topic of sickness is quite broad. One kind of sickness, for example, is the flu. In his article about the 2017–2018 flu season, Patrick May with *The Mercury News* talks about the unique spread of that season's flu: "In every pocket of the continental United States, people are experiencing flu symptoms right now, the first time that has happened in the 13 years of the CDC's current tracking system.... The rate of flu hospitalizations . . . nearly doubled earlier this month from 13.7 one week to 22.7 the next."[1]

---

[1] Patrick May, "This flu epidemic did something never recorded before," *The Mercury News*, last modified January 29, 2018, https://www.mercurynews.com/2018/01/15/stories-from-a-nation-full-of-flu-sufferers.

Another kind of sickness is plague. In the fourteenth century, Europe, as well as the rest of the world, suffered massive casualties under the Black Plague. At that time in history, the world's population was approximately 450 million, and estimates of plague-related deaths range from 75 million all the way up to 200 million. Some historians say that as much as half of Europe's population may have died out in just four years.[2]

Long before the Black Plague arrived on the scene, there was Justinian's Plague in AD 542.[3] This plague killed approximately 25 million people. Modern scholars estimate that at one point during the outbreak nearly five thousand people per day died in Constantinople. The plague advanced so quickly through the city, killing so many, that bodies were left in piles in public streets. Clean-up crews simply could not keep up with the death toll.

Lest we think plagues were problems of the past while we only deal with flus now, look at what the World Health Organization (WHO) says about AIDS: "Since the beginning of the epidemic, more than 70 million people have been infected with the HIV virus and about 35 million people have died of HIV."[4]

The death tolls of these plagues are staggering, and they include men, women, and children. Every time we think we have eliminated a sickness, or even actually eliminated an

---

[2] "The Five Deadliest Outbreaks and Pandemics in History," Culture of Health Blog, published December 16, 2013, https://www.rwjf.org/en/culture-of-health/2013/12/the_five_deadliesto.html.
[3] John Horgan, "Justinian's Plague (541-542 CE)," Ancient History Encyclopedia, published December 26, 2014, https://www.ancient.eu/article/782/justinians-plague-541-542-ce/.
[4] "HIV/AIDS," Global Health Observatory (GHO) data, World Health Organization, accessed January 17, 2018, http://www.who.int/gho/hiv/en/.

outbreak, another one takes its place in rather short order. Scientists and medical professionals may be able to determine the root cause of a disease with much effort and funding, but that does not stop new outbreaks or mutations of old ones. We keep developing cures and treatments, but new sicknesses keep coming up.

What if we were to go a step further? What if we were to consider some of the other problems beside the flu, plagues, and AIDS, which are at least diagnosable? There are other conditions that cannot be accurately diagnosed, treated, or cured.

What about the many instances of chronic pain that remain regardless of treatment? Laura Kiesel writes the following about chronic pain in a *Harvard Health Publishing* article for Harvard Medical School:

> In 2011, a study by the Institute of Medicine discovered that pain can endure long after the illness or injury that caused its initial onset has been treated or healed, until it eventually evolves, or devolves, into its own disease. That is, pain is no longer indicative of another prognosis—it is the prognosis, and a disabling one at that. . . . Most medical students are woefully lacking in training in chronic pain, usually receiving only a few hours' worth in their entire education. In fact, veterinarians receive more training on how to treat animals in pain than medical doctors do for their human patients.[5]

What about those who suffer from insomnia, or sleeplessness? Insomnia can last for less than a week to more than

---

[5] Laura Kiesel, "Chronic pain: The 'invisible' disability," *Harvard Health Publishing*, published April 28, 2017, https://www.health.harvard.edu/blog/chronic-pain-the-invisible-disability-2017042811360.

a decade. It can even be a progressive neurodegenerative disease that proves fatal.[6] According to the US Centers for Disease Control (CDC), insufficient sleep is a public health epidemic.[7] In fact, one-third of adult Americans report some degree of insomnia.[8] Insomnia can lead to health conditions such as heart attack, coronary heart disease, stroke, asthma, COPD, cancer, arthritis, chronic kidney disease, and more.[9]

What's the deal here? Regardless of the money, time, and effort we pour into eliminating sicknesses and disease, it keeps coming. But from where did all this come? What is the basic cause of sickness? Dr. Robert D. Smith answers that question for us by looking not to the medical but to the theological. He says, "The basic cause of all illness is the curse of sin on all mankind resulting from the fall of Adam."[10] Dr. Smith correctly points us toward the cause of all sickness: sin.

---

[6] "Fatal familial insomnia," Diseases, Genetic and Rare Diseases Information Center, accessed February 15, 2018, https://rarediseases.info.nih.gov/diseases/6429/fatal-familial-insomnia.
[7] Ginger Pinholster, "Sleep Deprivation Described as a Serious Public Health Problem," AAAS, March 14, 2014, https://www.aaas.org/news/sleep-deprivation-described-serious-public-health-problem.
[8] "Sleep and Sleep Disorders," Centers for Disease Control and Prevention, CDC 24/7: Saving Lives, Protecting People, last updated February 22, 2018, https://www.cdc.gov/sleep/index.html.
[9] "Short Sleep Duration Among US Adults," Data and Statistics, Centers for Disease Control and Prevention, CDC 24/7: Saving Lives, Protecting People, last updated May 2, 2017, https://www.cdc.gov/sleep/data_statistics.html.
[10] Robert D. Smith, MD, *The Christian Counselor's Medical Desk Reference* (Stanley, NC: Timeless Texts, 2000), 27.

1

Categories of Causality

THE ROOT CAUSE OF ALL SICKNESS falls in one of two categories: directly, as the curse for sin, and indirectly, as the result of sin. Viewing sickness through the lens of original causality can help clarify the relationship between sickness and disobedience and between health and obeying God, but as we will see as we dive deeper into the categories of causality, there is also danger in seeking to judge the lives of others based on their apparent health or lack thereof.

The Curse for Sin

The first category is God's curse against sin. Let's look at the first causal category of sickness, the curse on all mankind brought on by sin. Ultimately, our sickness is our fault. We sinned against God. He was gracious by not immediately killing mankind and instead cursing him, along with the rest of the created order.

In Genesis 2:17, mankind—that is, Adam and Eve—had yet to sin. They were living in a state of innocence, untested holiness. God then gave man the responsibility of abstaining from the Tree of the Knowledge of Good and Evil. It was by obeying this command that Adam could demonstrate his faith and trust in God. In obeying God, Adam and Eve would live in peace with Him.

However, the consequence for failing to obey God's command was death. Adam failed to obey God. As the head and representative of all mankind, Adam came under the curse of sin as a deadly consequence to his disobedience. Remember, God had warned Adam that in the day he eats from the forbidden tree, he "shall surely die." The curse of sin is death. Therefore, all mankind came under the curse of sin in both an eternal and temporal sense, just as Adam.

Regardless of our thoughts, desires, beliefs, or intentions, every single person, because of sin's curse, will become sick on their way to death. Ezekiel 18:4, 20 says, "Behold, all souls are Mine; the soul of the father as well as the soul of the son is Mine. *The soul who sins will die. . . . The person who sins will die.* The son will not bear the punishment for the father's iniquity, nor will the father bear the punishment for the son's iniquity; the righteousness of the righteous will be upon himself, and the wickedness of the wicked will be upon himself" (italics mine).[1]

---

1 Note that these verses dispel the fallacious notion some have of a generational curse. Some use Ex. 20:5–6 to try to assert that they are sick or "addicted" to a substance or behavior due to a generational curse as if they were a helpless victim. However, the prophet was teaching personal responsibility and culpability before Yahweh for one's own sin. The idea of the father's sin being upon the third and fourth generation of children simply means that, if not dealt with, the father's sin would indeed be imbibed by the children. They would practice the same idolatry and God-hating as their fathers and teach it to the next generation. Sinful thoughts and actions spread from one generation to the next, but thanks be to the Lord that His mercy to His people surpasses that to thousands of generations.

Death is a direct result of sin's curse. Each individual person will get sick and die because each person has a sin nature, has sinned, and is under the curse of sin. In speaking to this truth, Wayne Grudem says that death came about "by the entrance of sin into the world."[2]

Since all people live under the curse of sin, all people are in the process of dying. Sickness is part of the process of dying. The ongoing process of dying is a daily, unavoidable deterioration of one's body. Death and sickness affect both Christians and non-Christians. There may even be physical conditions, to various degrees, that no doctor can accurately diagnose or treat. People in a sin-cursed world get sick, diseased, and eventually die in a variety of ways. Sin is the basic cause of our sickness and death.

The Results of Sin

The second causal category deals with the results of sin and answers the question of how sin's curse and resulting sickness can manifest themselves in an individual's life. The general answer is that the manifestation, or result, could be due to the person sinning or the person being sinned against. While we consider sin and sickness in a person's life, we ought to also keep in mind that it is not for us to speculate in the life of another. We do not want to be like Job's useless counselors and assume that another's sickness is directly tied to personal rebellion. That simply may not be the case. Yet in this context of learning about the relationship of sin and sickness, we are going to consider the possible connections.

---

[2] Wayne A. Grudem, *Systematic Theology: An Introduction to Biblical Doctrine* (Leicester, England; Grand Rapids, MI: InterVarsity; Zondervan, 2004), 1239.

2

Aspects of Causality

Within the general answer above, we have some specific aspects to consider. In fact, the issue of sin causing sickness in a person's life has four different aspects. In each, God has a sovereign purpose for the sickness (see Rom. 8:28–29). To have a biblical understanding of why we might get sick, let's look at four aspects of sickness in a person's life.

Punishment or Chastening

First, God may sovereignly use sickness as punishment for sin in the nonbeliever or as chastening for the believer. Let's consider three examples of this truth. Exodus 15:26 says, "And He said, 'If you will give earnest heed to the voice of the Lord your God, and do what is right in His sight, and give ear to His commandments, and keep all His statutes, I will put none of the diseases on you which I have put on the Egyptians; for I, the Lord, am your healer.'" God punished the unbelieving nation of Egypt with severe plagues. But here God explicitly promises to not punish the people of Israel if they obey Him. At the same time, stated implicitly, He would indeed chasten His people with sickness and disease should they disobey.

In 2 Samuel 12:14-15, Nathan says to David, "'However, because by this deed you have given occasion to the enemies of the Lord to blaspheme, the child also that is born to you shall surely die.' So Nathan went to his house. Then the Lord struck the child that Uriah's widow bore to David, so that he was very sick." Because David chose to value sin over God, he reaped the consequences. The child he and Uriah's wife bore out of a murderous and adulterous affair was struck with illness and eventually died as an infant. Furthermore, if we keep reading the narrative, we would see that as a consequence to his sin, David's family life was tumultuous and disastrous. Sin is indeed dangerous and deadly, and its consequences do not always stay confined to the offender.

In 1 Corinthians 11:27-30, Paul warns believers about partaking of the Lord's Table in an unworthy manner: "Therefore whoever eats the bread or drinks the cup of the Lord in an unworthy manner, shall be guilty of the body and the blood of the Lord. But let a man examine himself, and so let him eat of the bread and drink of the cup. For he who eats and drinks, eats and drinks judgment to himself, if he does not judge the body rightly. For this reason many among you are weak and sick, and a number sleep."

Individuals in the Corinthian church were partaking of the Lord's Supper with unaddressed sin. The offending members were not repenting from their sin and were taking Christ's sacrifice lightly. That's sinful and offensive to God. Therefore,

He saw fit to chastise some with sickness and weakness, while He put to death other more serious offenders to purify His church. God has chastened and punished people with sickness and death and will continue to do so (see Heb. 12:4–7; Acts 5:1–11; Ps. 32, 51).

Repentance

Second, God may sovereignly use sickness to produce repentance. In the next example He did just that. Historically, God used sickness to lead ancient Israel out of sin and into repentance. While we are not ancient Israel, the universal principle is that God will use sickness to produce repentance. In Numbers 21:5–7, Moses writes,

> And the people spoke against God and Moses, "Why have you brought us up out of Egypt to die in the wilderness? For there is no food and no water, and we loathe this miserable food." And the LORD sent fiery serpents among the people and they bit the people, so that many people of Israel died. So the people came to Moses and said, "We have sinned, because we have spoken against the LORD and you; intercede with the LORD, that He may remove the serpents from us." And Moses interceded for the people.

Let's make a few observations about the context and the text itself. In this context, the first generation of Israel is wandering in the wilderness. They were a disobedient and unbelieving generation. In fact, they were so disobedient that only two men, Joshua and Caleb, from this first generation made it into the promised land.

These Israelites lived in a perpetual cycle of disobedience, divine chastening, and repentance. Chapters 11 to 25 are filled with this cyclical disobedience, and in our text, they have renewed their complaints against the Lord while on their journey. It is by examining their complaint and the Lord's reaction that we will see the seriousness of Israel's rebellion and what He did to produce repentance.

In 21:1 we see that Israel suffered an attack by the king of Arad, and the text informs us that he even took some Israelite prisoners. In response to King Arad's aggressive actions, Israel asked the Lord to help them "utterly destroy" the king, his forces, and his cities (v. 2). So, out of His graciousness, the Lord answered Israel's request, so that the Canaanites and their cities were, as the text repeats, "utterly destroyed" (v. 3). At this point the Israelites should have been amazed at how the Lord enabled them to overcome their enemies. They did not simply beat them in battle—they *utterly destroyed* them, and not just one city but several cities.

However, the Israelites' gratitude toward the Lord was not forthcoming. In verse 4, after their divinely enabled victory, they set out on their journey to the promised land once again, but they believed they had a problem. The route they were to take from their current location of Mount Hor to go around Edom was a longer route, and the Israelites thought this route was unacceptable. The text says that they "became impatient because of the journey." Israel had received from the Lord what they requested, and immediately afterward, they find something that does not fit their desires. Israel had a test set before them: a longer route. When they learned of the route to take, they could have trusted the Lord's leading and followed it. Lest we forget, this is the same Lord who had just led them through a victorious battle. Yet they chose to rebel against Him. They thought the Lord chose a needlessly lengthened route, and they became impatient. The Israelites' hearts were not right. So in verse 5, out of their hearts their mouths spoke. Moses said that "the people spoke against God and Moses."

We should notice a critical transition here. In verses 2 and 7, Moses writes that the people address God as "Lord," which is the English translation of the name Yahweh. *Yahweh* indicates the covenant God of Israel. It is acknowledging the righteous, loving, and kind character of their God. It is saying that He is a promise-maker and keeper to Israel. There is an intimacy in relationship attached to the name Yahweh. Yet in verse 5, the Israelites "spoke against God." There is a difference here. The word *God* is the English translation of the title Elohim. *Elohim* pointed to God as Creator and Judge of the universe. While that is certainly true—God is the Creator and Judge—it lacks the intimacy of the name Yahweh. Although it is not wrong to refer to the Lord as God, in this context it is actually an evolution of their sinful thinking.

This is the difference—in this context, it is like seeing your father as righteous, good, truthful, intimate, and the standard which to follow versus seeing him as the male figurehead and disciplinarian. A change in the relationship has entered Israel's mind. They have moved from the intimacy of addressing by name to addressing by title. They have moved away from Yahweh to God. They are building a case in their heart against the Lord.

The progression is that they first became impatient. Their thoughts were prideful. They figured they had a better route. *Who cares about the war victory? That's in the past. This ridiculous journey before us is now.* Then, in their thinking, they distanced themselves from Yahweh to God. They must have thought He was unfair. He was not giving them what they wanted—a short journey. No, He was dragging them all over the place by way of a longer journey around Edom. After mulling this over in their minds, they couldn't take it anymore. They had to do something! So, out of their hearts their mouths spoke against God. God had to be set straight. He had to hear what they had to say to Him through His man, Moses. The word "spoke" used here in verse 5 indicates some kind of threat that they were repeating over and over. They were threatening God, by way of Moses, about the longer journey. They were not accepting the idea of a longer route. They wanted a shorter, and surely much "wiser," route.

In their minds this longer route was designed by a distant Creator and Judge to slowly kill them. This was not the Yahweh who gave them the promises and who had just led them out of battle. No, this is a distant deity who creates then cruelly judges His creation. We know they were thinking this way not just because of their impatience but also because of their verbal complaint.

Their criticism was of a presuppositional nature. In the form of a pointed question, it actually accuses the Lord. They asked, "Why have you brought us up out of Egypt to die in the wilderness?" Notice they are assuming the Lord's motives and accusing Him based on that assumption. They are coming to the table with a verdict in their mind concerning the Lord. They assume He is guilty of genocidal actions on an innocent nation. They said "*You* brought us up out of Egypt..." (italics mine). They are saying that God actively took them out of where they were (Egypt) and brought them to where they are now. That is true; however, they are willfully forgetting that He rescued them out of slavery in Egypt. It was a divine mercy and an act of grace that He took them out of

Egypt. Yet they are now claiming it wasn't due to the Lord's mercy and graciousness that He delivered them out of Egypt but because He had cruel intentions. *No, God is not kind. He's cruel and even murderous. He brought us out here to starve to death* (v. 5).

Lastly, in their downward, sinful spiral in their case against the Lord, Israel tries to make God a liar. They claim "there is no food and no water." This is an interesting claim, as the Lord had just miraculously provided water out of a rock in 20:11. In fact, it was enough water for the nation and their livestock. And at the end of 21:5 they said, "We loathe this miserable food." So they did have food and water. How could they claim, on one hand, they had no food and water, but, on the other, they did have food and water? It's pretty simple. Just as a child throws a temper tantrum when there are no snacks according to his or her desire and yet there is a pantry full of food, so it is with Israel.

The Israelites had plenty of food and water, and they knew it. They just wanted to multiply the accusations against the Lord to build their case against Him. The food they loathed was the manna the Lord had provided from heaven. Interestingly, the Hebrew word for both occurrences of "food" in this verse is the same word: *lahem*. This speaks to the point made earlier—they had food; they just wanted *different* food. They were ungrateful. In fact, they were so ungrateful of the food the Lord had provided that they would rather go about the laborious process of making their own bread after harvesting their own wheat. The Lord's life-sustaining bread was simply not good enough for them. They hated the Lord's provision down to the very depths of their soul. They found His gracious provision dreadful and disgusting. Their opinion of the

Lord's provision was so low that they didn't even count it as food. According to them, God was distant and cruel and was actively leading them to die by means of a death march and starvation in the desert.

It is for this rebellion that the Lord sent sickness and death to them (v. 6). The Lord had to punish their sin, and yet, He had their repentance in mind too. The means the Lord used to accomplish this was to send poisonous snakes among the people. The bite of these snakes caused intense pain by way of burning inflammation. The poison was so potent and the inflammation so severe that "many people of Israel died." This scenario was divinely designed by God to be terrifying—and to bring about repentance.

We will see that repentance is exactly what was accomplished. Moses says in the beginning of verse 7, "So the people came to Moses." Repentance is a change in mind (i.e., the will) that leads to a change in action and speech, and that is what we see here. In verse 5 Israel "spoke against" God and Moses, but now they "came to" Moses, God's man. A change in their minds led to a 180 degree change in their actions. Before they went away from the Lord; now they came to Him. We are seeing a put off/put on process at work because of God's chastening.

The Israelites confessed their sin specifically. They told Moses, "We have sinned, because we have spoken against the Lord and you." After Israel received their severe chastening from the Lord, they changed their tune. The case they were building against Him is now rightly confessed as sin.

Notice another change in Israel. Their speech has changed. They have moved from referring to the Lord by title—God— and are back to calling Him by His covenant name—Yahweh.

The pain has shown them the error of their ways. They are submitting to and desiring a restoration of relational intimacy with Yahweh because the pain of rebellion is too much to bear. The fiery trials were way too horrifying and costly. They were thinking, Let's turn from the wrong idea of a distant, male-figurehead disciplinarian back to a good and righteous covenant keeper. They knew they were wrong, they experienced the deadly consequences, and now they are repenting. They are desirous of reconciliation with the Lord.

In verses 8 and 9, the Lord gave Moses the remedy for their punishment. Moses was to make a bronze serpent and set it on a pole. Then, whenever someone was bitten, he was to look at the fiery serpent on the pole, and he would live. In other words, the Israelites had to employ their will to take advantage of the Lord's prescription. They had to trust the Lord's way, not their own. They had to willfully look "to the bronze serpent." In this way, the Lord cared enough about His and His people's holiness to severely chasten His people so they would be brought to repentance.

For another example of this principle, look at 1 Corinthians 5:5. In regard to an unrepentant professing believer in the church, Paul says to "deliver such a one to Satan for the destruction of his flesh, that his spirit may be saved in the day of the Lord Jesus."

God takes the holiness of His church seriously. He also takes it seriously when someone makes a profession of faith in His name. In this context, the apostle Paul, whose desires were for a pure church and repentance from sin, exercised his God-given authority to excommunicate an immoral man, a so-called brother in Christ (vv. 1, 11). Due to this man's sin, Paul effectively put him out of the blessing and protection of the body of Christ by thrusting him out of the church and into the world's wicked system (i.e., Satan's realm).

Furthermore, Paul said that this was for "the destruction of his flesh" (v. 5). Here Paul is referring to God's chastening in the form of sickness even leading to death. This may seem harsh, but the purity of the church was and is the priority. Alongside the purity of the church is the hope for the purification of the excommunicated church member (v. 5).

Now, why should the church do this? Sure, we know the purity of the church is crucial. At the same time, how is this action—thrusting this man out of the church—effective in bringing about his repentance? A much greater possibility exists that the pain and consequences God uses to chasten him outside the church will drive him to repentance more effectively than any state of comfort and ease inside the church. God's severe disciplining, which can destroy the body, is meant to produce a heart of repentance. Is our God-ordained sickness, in fact, God driving us toward repentance? It would be wise for us to humbly and prayerfully consider this possibility and ask the Lord to reveal sin in our heart (see also Ps. 19:12–13).

Natural Consequences

A third way sickness is used sovereignly in a person's life is as a natural consequence. God has ordained sickness or death as a result of the natural consequences of sin. In this case, sickness, injury, and even death come from violating the natural laws God has put in place. It should be said that several ideas are floating around in the world about natural law. Some are legitimate while others are not. In this section we will only focus on one kind of natural law. For us to have a sharp focus on the specific natural law we are considering, let's look at what is and is not being discussed.

We are not talking about laws of nature in the sense that many intimate as Mother Nature. Neither are we speaking of nature as a self-aware being who made laws we all obey. We are not referring to jurisprudence or to natural law, which holds universally that law should be based on morality and ethics (even though that is true).[1] Lastly, we are not discussing the revealed law of God in the sense of the Decalogue or the natural law in Romans 2:14 that is written on the hearts of Gentiles and holds them accountable to God.[2]

Rather, we are discussing the laws of nature God has imposed on His creation—laws such as logic, physics, and order through which He upholds and sustains His universe. We are talking about the laws of how things work that were imposed by God at the time of creation. If these laws didn't exist, there would be no predictability and no repeatable observations. But they do exist, so we do have predictability and repeatable observations. Since creation and the laws that God gave to govern its normative function are so grand, we ought to take time to think about the absolute awe and wonder of God's creative act.

People like to think highly of themselves. They like to tout their scientific prowess and accumulated knowledge. Yet the fact is it has taken man an embarrassingly long time to catch up to one of the first truths God has taught. It has taken mankind thousands of years to understand what God did in the

---

[1] "Natural Law," All About Philosophy, accessed April 11, 2018, https://www.allaboutphilosophy.org/natural-law.htm.
[2] F. L. Cross and E. A. Livingstone, eds., *The Oxford Dictionary of the Christian Church*, 3rd ed. rev., (Oxford; New York: Oxford University Press, 2005), 1139.

beginning—the creation of our physical reality—and later recorded in His Word.

As an example, we can take the acclaimed scientist Herbert Spencer (1820–1903). Spencer was an English philosopher, biologist, anthropologist, sociologist, and liberal political theorist—and an unbeliever. He was an intellectual elite who had won many awards for his scientific achievements. But his greatest success was in discovering the categories of the knowable.[3] Spencer taught that everything fits into one of five categories: time, force, action, space, matter. For this discovery, he was hailed by the scientific community.

However, as groundbreaking as this was, it was completely elementary in concept and late upon arrival. We know this because in Genesis 1:1 God had already made these categories about six thousand years prior to Spencer. The text in Genesis 1:1 says, "In the beginning [time] God [force] created [action] the heavens [space] and the earth [matter]."

What took man thousands of years to categorize, due to its massive complexity, God had simply communicated in one sentence. Now, it is worth stating that the Bible is not a science textbook. However, when it makes scientific—or any other—claims, it is always accurate, authoritative, and true. At the time of creation, God gave us the laws we could use to scientifically study, or observe, our universe. Boiled down, a working definition of science is this: the observation of things. Without the laws God gave us, we couldn't observe things with any certainty.

Now, these laws, as secular science wrongly postulates, did not occur at the Big Bang for at least two reasons. The first

---

[3] "The Theology of Creation," 90-359, Selected Scriptures, Sermons, Grace to You, published August 24, 2008, https://www.gty.org/library/sermons-library/90-359/the-theology-of-creation.

reason is because the big bang is scientifically impossible. Physically speaking, it is impossible to get something from nothing, and that is exactly what the big bang theory claims to have happened. The theory basically states that first there was nothing, an explosion happened, and out of it came everything that exists.

This theory then teaches that out of all the spontaneously created matter, which was in a chaotic and random state, order began to arise over the course of billions of years. But the second law of thermodynamics works to the contrary. It basically says that the life of things begins at order and ends in disorder. In other words, things go from order to chaos, not the other way around.

An example of this law at work would be watching the process of a building being demolished. First, there is a building, then demolition crews strategically insert explosives around the building's foundation. Then, after everyone has cleared to a safe distance, the explosives are ignited. What do we see once this happens? The building falls down into a pile of rubble. That is the second law of thermodynamics at work. There was an orderly building that had been carefully planned out and constructed. Then, an explosion happened. Next, there is no building, only a pile of debris. Everything just went from order to disorder, or chaos. Never has anyone blown up a pile of rubble and beheld a building when the dust cleared. That is scientifically impossible no matter how many times one blows up the rubble.

Further complicating that theory for secular scientists is the fact that they have no witnesses. In the case of the big bang theory, it is not observable or repeatable. It is not observational science. Christians, however, have an easier time explaining the origin of the universe. The answer is in Genesis

1:1, which says, "In the beginning God created the heavens and the earth." In that one sentence we have an eyewitness of the creative act, none other than the Creator Himself. God, through Moses, communicates in His Word the fact that He created the universe. Furthermore, God's creative act is verifiable and historically repeatable. One can read Genesis 1:1 as many times as they desire, observing what happened. It will always have the same outcome. It will always come back to "God created."

The second reason these laws did not occur at the big bang is because a naturalistic process cannot create laws that are immaterial. It does not matter the size of the explosion—there will be no laws of logic formulated by it. That is an impossibility. The physical cannot create the immaterial.

God, who is orderly and does not change, created immaterial laws that also do not change. They did not come about by a naturalistic process. God created these laws to uphold and sustain His created physical universe, to make it habitable by physical creatures, to make it knowable through observation, and to bring Himself glory. In fact, the five categories above are only observable because of God's natural laws. God brings Himself glory through His natural laws because they govern the creation that points to the Creator.

Speaking to the reason and reality of why God has put natural laws in place, Dr. Jason Lisle says,

> Natural laws exist because the universe has a Creator God who is logical and has imposed order on His universe (Genesis 1:1). . . . Everything in the universe, every plant and animal, every rock, every particle of matter or light wave, is bound by laws which it has no choice but to obey. The Bible tells us that there are laws

of nature—"ordinances of heaven and earth" (Jeremiah 33:25) These laws describe the way God normally accomplishes His will in the universe.

God's logic is built into the universe, and so the universe is not haphazard or arbitrary. It obeys laws of chemistry that are logically derived from the laws of physics, many of which can be logically derived from other laws of physics and laws of mathematics. The most fundamental laws of nature exist only because God wills them to; they are the logical, orderly way that the Lord upholds and sustains the universe He has created.[1]

We need to get this idea. God has put natural laws in place that our physical reality has "no choice but to obey." God has done this to uphold and sustain our universe. God has created the universe, and He has determined how it works. He has made unchanging laws intertwined with His creation to govern its operation, and there are consequences for breaking those laws.

With that being said, let's look at a couple examples of natural consequences to God's natural laws being broken and the resulting consequences. The first illustration is of someone with explosive anger. They get mad and strike an object that is harder than their hand. Since the object being struck is harder than the hand used in striking, the hand will break when employed with sufficient force. God didn't break the hand. The person, who failed to control his anger, broke his hand. He failed to observe the natural law set in place by God (i.e., Newton's third recognized law [action-reaction]) and, consequently, broke his hand. The individual's lack of self-control, not God or the wall or even Sir Isaac Newton, is to blame.

---

[1] Jason Lisle, "God & Natural Law," *Answers*, Answers in Genesis, published August 28, 2006, https://answersingenesis.org/is-god-real/god-natural-law.

Not surprisingly, we can align the above example with God's natural laws observed in Genesis 1:1. In other words, we can run the example through the five categories God gave us and Spencer recognized to see how these five categories of law work. If we recount the hypothetical scenario, it would go thusly: when [time] this person [force] got angry and swung [action] his hand [matter] toward [space] the harder wall [more matter] and broke his hand, it was because he failed to obey the natural laws God had set in place for his sustainment.

As another example, an individual, whom we will call Steve, chooses to use illegal drugs. Steve shares a needle with a fellow user, whom we will call Tom. Unknown to Tom, Steve has a communicable disease. When Tom uses Steve's needle, Tom also contracts the disease.

In this scenario Tom now has a communicable disease because he made sinful choices that led to drug enslavement (likewise for Steve). Tom further complicated the matter by choosing to share a needle with another user in order to get high. Tom is reaping the consequences of the sinful choices he sowed. Tom's natural barrier against such a disease, the epidermis and dermis, failed to protect him from the disease because he chose to defeat that barrier with a used hypodermic needle. Tom, not Steve or the drug or the drug delivery system, is to blame.

Other examples of natural consequences due to sin are liver damage from enslavement to alcohol, kidney damage from enslavement to various drugs, vehicular homicide from drunk driving, cancer from smoking, dental problems from grinding or clenching teeth during anger or anxiety, heart disease or muscular atrophy brought on by excessive laziness.

The examples of natural consequences could be multiplied many times over. God put natural laws in place for the purpose of His own glorification, protection of people, and to aid human flourishing. Breaking God's natural laws has consequences. We ought to seriously ask and evaluate whether we are sick or injured because we have broken one of God's laws.

Wrong Thinking

God has sovereignly ordained sickness as a result of unbiblical thinking and attitudes on the body. To help us better understand this truth, let's consider why people think the way they do about life, briefly looking at two terms, their definitions, some examples, and how this all relates to us. Hopefully, at the end of this section we will have a better grasp of what the opening statement means and how to apply it.

With that purpose in mind, the first term we will consider is *worldview*. So, what is a worldview? A worldview is an overall, philosophical view of the world. It is an all-encompassing perspective on everything that exists and matters to us.[2] In other words, our worldview is how we perceive and answer all questions in life. Our worldview, like a pair of sunglasses, colors the way we interpret life. And everybody has a worldview, whether they have thought about it or not.

Since this is true of worldviews, an important question ought to be asked of them. What are worldviews based on, or how are they formed? All worldviews are based on or formed by presuppositions. A presupposition is a thing tacitly assumed at the beginning of a line of argument or course of

---

2 James Anderson, "What Is a Worldview?" Ligonier Ministries, published June 21, 2017, https://www.ligonier.org/blog/what-worldview.

action. In other words, a presupposition, even if unspoken, is a belief one holds to prior to making an argument or committing an action that directs the thought process of the argument and action. John MacArthur defines presuppositions as "beliefs that one presumes to be true without supporting independent evidence from other sources or systems. Interpreting reality, in part or in whole, requires that one adopt an interpretive stance since there is no 'neutral' thought in the universe. This becomes the foundation upon which one builds."[3]

Our presuppositions make up our worldview, and everybody has them. No one is neutral, whether a believer or an unbeliever. Everybody has a presuppositional stance that undergirds their worldview. So, is there a difference between a believer's and an unbeliever's presuppositional stance? Yes, there is a huge difference. And that difference is the source of authority. Let's make some comparisons between the believer's and unbeliever's source of authority and how that can manifest during a trial in life, since everybody has those too.

The believer's source of authority is God's revealed word in Scripture. The believer presupposes Scripture to be true and authoritative (John 17:17). The believer believes God's Word because of the supernatural faith received from God (Eph. 2:8–9).

In contrast, an unbeliever's source of authority, in its many forms, is himself (Rom. 8:6–8). Whether it is in the form of atheism or a false religion, the unbeliever's source of authority always resides in self. The unbeliever willfully presupposes Scripture to not be true or authoritative (Rom. 1:18). The

---

[3] John F. MacArthur and Richard Mayhue, *Think Biblically!* (Wheaton, IL: Crossway, 2003), 13.

unbeliever believes, at the end of the day, his own authority, by assumed faith. In other words, the unbeliever's presuppositions are assumed as correct based on his willful assumption that he is the most capable and correct authority in his life.[4]

Therefore, when trials arise in both an unbeliever's and a believer's life, a different response occurs by each type of person. So then, let's make another comparison. First, when a trial arises in a believer's life, if he or she thinks consistently with a biblical worldview, they will find peace within the midst of the trial because God is at the center of their worldview. We will look at this truth more closely a little later.

But what happens when unbelievers face trials in their lives? When a trial arises in an unbeliever's life, if they think consistently with an unbiblical worldview, they will experience a lack of peace. Their life will be "hard" (Prov. 13:15).

We are not saying that unbelievers cannot be trained to greater levels of self-control in difficult circumstances—the world is replete with examples of this. We can look no further than the trained soldier who can keep his cool in the battlefield. Bullets can be whizzing past their head, yet they can remain in control enough to consider a plan of action and execute it, thanks to their training.

Nonetheless, no unbeliever on the planet will have the same kind of heart responses to trials as a believer. No unbeliever can be both sorrowful to the core and joyful to the core at the same time. Only a believer can hold both a deep sorrow and joy simultaneously, because only a believer has Christ

---

4 This presupposition fails to recognize the noetic effects of sin, his sin nature, and the god of this world who blinds his mind to the truth (see Isa. 53:6; Rom. 8:3; 1 John 1:8; 2 Cor. 4:4).

as their authority and source of joy. So even though the trial may be deep down, dirty, and even deadly, the believer knows it cannot separate him or her from the love of Christ because Scripture says so (Rom. 8:35–39). An unbeliever does not have that promise from God because he refuses to submit to Him or believe His Word (Rom. 8:5–8). Thus, an unbeliever and a believer will each have a much different view of what happens to them in life because their respective worldviews affect the conclusions to their observations in life.

How does our worldview affect the conclusions to our observations? We all have the same evidence to observe. There is not one set of evidence for believers and a different set for unbelievers. We all have the same evidence around us to observe. It is not a question of evidence but a question of *interpretation* of the evidence, and that interpretation is colored by the worldview to which one ascribes.

We can see how this truth works, for example, when we consider the fossil record. Secular scientists view the same fossil record (the evidence) that believing scientists observe. Both sets of scientists see the same evidence. They both ascertain that there are billions of dead things buried in rock layers, scattered all over the earth. However, the conclusion of the secular scientist, due in part to the fossil record, is that the earth is millions of years old.

Many times, in order to reach the conclusion of millions of years, secular scientists use the carbon-14 dating method. Yet this is a problematic dating method when it comes to long spans of time because the element is very unstable and quickly changes into nitrogen. In fact, the half-life of the carbon-14 element is 5,730 years. Therefore, if fossils were really millions of years old, as secular-thinking scientists claim, there would be no carbon-14 left in them to test! Speaking on this fact, Dr. Andrew A. Snelling says,

> Radiocarbon (carbon-14) is a very unstable element that quickly changes into nitrogen. Half the original quantity of carbon-14 will decay back to the stable element nitrogen-14 after only 5,730 years. (This 5,730-year period is called the half-life of radiocarbon. . . . At this decay rate, hardly any carbon-14 atoms will remain after only 57,300 years (or ten half-lives) . . . . So if fossils are really millions of years old, as evolutionary scientists claim, no carbon-14 atoms would be left in them. Indeed, if all the atoms making up the entire earth were radiocarbon, then after only 1 million years absolutely no carbon-14 atoms should be left![5]

Given the measurable fact above, how can secular-thinking scientists come up with millions of years? The answer is both simple and sad. They twist the facts and evidence. Their worldview, the glasses through which they view the world around them, colors or interprets their conclusions to the evidence. They suppress the truth about creation, its Creator, and the consequences, and they lead many astray in unrighteousness. Thus, they are storing up God's wrath for themselves (Rom. 1:18; 2:5). They think there is no divine Authority, no God (Ps. 10:4; 14:1). They hold to their own natural ability to discern what is true and false—that is, they are their own authority.

However, when believing scientists observe the same evidence—the fossil record—they have a completely different conclusion. They think about the global flood and remember

---

[5] Andrew A. Snelling, "Carbon-14 in Fossils and Diamonds: An Evolution Dilemma," *Answers*, Answers in Genesis, published January 1, 2011, https://answersingenesis.org/geology/carbon-14/carbon-14-in-fossils-and-diamonds.

that the Bible says God judged the world through a cataclysmic global flooding event (Gen. 7; 2 Peter 3:5–6). Their presupposition is that the Bible is true. Therefore, their worldview sees God's invisible hand at work in the fossil record. When coming to the fossil record, a believing scientist assumes that he or she should find billions of dead things buried in rock layers, scattered all over the earth by a global flood. And what exactly is found when the fossil record is viewed? What is the evidence one can observe? Billions of dead things buried in rock layers, scattered all over the earth. This is exactly what one would expect to find after a global flood ripped up miles of sediment, redepositing it in layers, while organisms got trapped and buried, turning into fossils.[6]

Yet secular scientists will reject that conclusion to the fossil record evidence even if they need to employ a scientifically unfit method to date the evidence (i.e., carbon-14) so it fits their desired narrative. Due to their presuppositional stance and resulting worldview, they reject rational conclusions and adopt irrational, sinful conclusions. They discard the truth in favor of a lie because, in their mind, their conclusions are authoritative and they ultimately hate the idea of God.

No amount of evidence will change the mind of an unbeliever. Regardless of the observable evidence, if the wrong worldview is employed, the interpretation of the evidence will likewise be wrong. In other words, because they refuse to see the truth, they will suppress the truth in unrighteousness (Rom. 1:18–19).

---

6 Ken Ham, "Billions of Dead Things: Five Reasons to Reject Millions of Years," Volume 123, Answers in Genesis, published November 16, 2016, https://answersingenesis.org/media/audio/answers-with-ken-ham/volume-123/billions-of-dead-things.

Now, how does all this relate to our topic at hand? A person's attitude, which is informed by their presuppositions and worldview, affects the body, like worldview affects conclusions to evidence. Your thinking, your presuppositions, can affect your body.

Let's work through this idea. If someone is atheistic, believes in the wrong god, or has a wrong view of the biblical God, then that will lead to unbiblical responses and wrong conclusions to the observable evidence, which can, and will, cause various unpleasant physiological symptoms. Furthermore, unbiblical thinking can even exacerbate existing diseases and biological conditions. Wrong conclusions to evidence have their consequences, and those are all God-ordained too.

Another question should be asked. How does this process happen in somebody? The Bible teaches that we are duplex beings (Rom. 7:22; 2 Cor. 4:16; Eph. 3:16). We are both immaterial soul, which cannot be seen, and material body, which can be seen by us and others. Scripture refers to the inner man as the heart, soul, mind, or spirit. It teaches that the inner man is the source of thoughts, feelings, and choices (Matt. 12:34; 15:18; Luke 6:45; Rom. 9:2; Heb. 4:12) and that the inner man is the real you God sees and interacts with (1 Sam. 16:7).[7]

Jesus explained that our speech and behavior are our body's reflection of our inner life (Luke 6:45). Scripture also demonstrates that our body responds to, or is influenced by, activity of the inner man with physiological changes (see Pss. 6:2; 31:10; 38:3; 102:5). Two examples of the inner man affecting

---

[7] Elyse Fitzpatrick and Laura Hendrickson, *Will Medicine Stop the Pain? Finding God's Healing for Depression, Anxiety, & Other Troubling Emotions* (Chicago: Moody, 2006), 25.

the outer man are those of anger and anxiety. If someone has thoughts of anger, that may produce a clenched fist or maybe grinding of the teeth. If someone has anxious thoughts, that may produce an elevated heart rate or blood pressure.

Now the influence can go the other way too. The outer man can affect the inner man. Two examples of that could be fatigue and hunger. A highly fatigued body can make it more difficult to love and serve others. When your day has absolutely shredded you and all you can think about is getting home and to bed, yet you walk in the front door and hear, "Daddy, Daddy, play with us," it can be a real challenge to your heart to serve others (Luke 17:7–9).

Likewise, being really hungry can make it more difficult to have patience with others. Recently, the word *hangry* has come into our nomenclature. Hangry means that someone has been so hungry for so long that they have become angry. The last thing someone in this position wants is something or someone standing between them and their food. In this scenario, patience is harder to choose because the stomach, the outer man, is trying to drive the inner man.

These concepts are not vastly different than a driver and vehicle scenario. The driver is not the car, and the car is not the driver. Yet each one can affect the other. The driver can be compared to the inner man, while the car could be compared to the outer man. The inner man can influence the car by stepping on a pedal or turning a steering wheel. The car can influence the driver by not responding properly to the pedals or steering wheel. Neither is the other, but each influences the other.

The inner man—the heart, mind, and soul—interacts with God. The thoughts, feelings, and choices from the inner man affect the outer man with measurable evidence such as facial expressions, speech, body language, heartbeat, blood pressure, and trembling. Those manifestations, as well as responses to outside stimuli, can in turn affect the inner man. It is a circuit of evidence, observation, and response or conclusion. That is a biblical view of people.

So then, how does the world view people? It views them with a materialistic mindset. In other words, materialists say that the material world is all there is—no unseen world, no inner man, no soul. Therefore, the brain, an organ of the physical body, is the source of thoughts, feelings, and choices, they say, and not the inner man, because there is no such thing. Thoughts, feelings, and choices from the brain's chemical reactions affect the outer person. Those with this worldview would be able to observe the same evidence of facial expressions, speech, body language, heartbeat, blood pressure, and trembling, except many of them would attribute it all to chemical reactions in the brain. Most would claim that a person is depressed, anxious, or psychotic and acts out of those states due to chemical imbalances in the brain, even though there is no empirical evidence on which to make this conclusion.[8] They would be suppressing the truth in unrighteousness. Their worldview doesn't allow for God, or at least a biblically accurate view of God.

However, the Bible clearly teaches that our invisible inner person, not our brain, is the source of our thoughts,

---

8   Mark L. Ruffalo, "On the Myth of the Chemical Imbalance. No, you don't have a chemical imbalance in your brain," The Myth of the Chemical Imbalance, On the Rocks, published October 27, 2017, https://reneweddesign.wordpress.com/2017/10/27/the-myth-of-the-chemical-imbalance. See also Red Blue, "PSYCHIATRISTS – No Cure," YouTube, February 27, 2013, https://youtu.be/366FB8_Ving.

intentions, emotions, and choices. That is not to say that the brain does not have chemicals or that those chemicals never change. But the brain's chemicals are not the prime mover of man; the soul is.

Before we look a little more closely at that, an aside ought to be mentioned. When we consider a biblical view of people, we should also remember that we all live in a sin-cursed world. Sometimes people who live in a sin-cursed world have organs that don't work normally. The brain is an organ. Sometimes brains do not work properly. Sometimes there are cognitive-perceptual difficulties with a person's brain due to disease. When we use the term *cognitive*, we simply mean the ability to think clearly. When we use the term *perceptual*, we mean the ability to perceive reality correctly. For example, if someone has legitimate hallucinations, they are not perceiving reality correctly.

Some examples of cognitive-perceptual (C-P) diseases and disorders are Alzheimer's disease, autism, frontal lobe stroke, dementia, and schizophrenia.[9] However, autism is only known to be on the cognitive side and does not produce hallucinations. People with C-P difficulties are more difficult to care for and may need special medications not intended for other people. They may also have error in judgment from physical impairment, leading to error in action. This is not necessarily willful sin but a misunderstanding of self and circumstances (i.e., inadvertent sin). People with C-P difficulties may have actions and responses that do not look normative

---

9 Jon Brock, "Autism diagnosis by brain scan? It's time for a reality check," *The Guardian*, published February 23, 2017, https://www.theguardian.com/science/head-quarters/2017/feb/23/autism-diagnosis-by-brain-scan-its-time-for-a-reality-check.

to others, and they may not be, but they are people just the same. It's just that they have greater challenges in life because of sin's curse. Great discernment and wisdom are required to help people with brain disorders. People with C-P difficulties need much love and compassion. It's not good that they sin, but it is good that the Bible speaks to sin. The Bible gives hope to sinners! Christ died for our inadvertent sins, too, and that gives real hope.

The above aside is a much larger topic than a simple parenthetical statement. It is more complicated than what has been mentioned, but there are biblical answers and hope to be given. The point was to briefly introduce us to the concept so we do not observe more challenging evidence and come to erroneous conclusions. With that having been said, let's look a little more closely at the biblical view of the inner and outer man and where the brain's chemicals fit into the picture.

In a biblical view of the inner and outer man, to account for the brain's chemical reactions in the equation, we can simply observe the evidence as it is. We have already seen that the inner man is the source of all thoughts, feelings, and choices. We have also seen that those thoughts, feelings, and choices can affect the outer man in a variety of observable and measurable ways. Next, we saw that the outer man and physiological problems can also affect the inner man, making it harder to obey the Lord. This is why we need the Lord interacting with the inner man. We need His Spirit empowering us to battle wrong thinking that affects the outer man as well as help in responding to physical stimuli so that we are pleasing to Him.

So, where do the brain's chemicals come into play? We can think of the brain as the link God gave us between the inner and outer man. The flow would go like this: The inner man has a particular thought or feeling, whether righteous or unrighteous, and those thoughts and feelings are received by the brain. The brain then has chemical reactions in relation to the thoughts and feelings. Then the brain and its chemicals mediate those thoughts and feelings to the outer man. Those thoughts and feelings are then manifested in the outer man by physical responses, which could be facial expressions, various aspects of speech (tone, volume, etc.), body language, elevated blood pressure, heart palpitations, and other physical responses. And it is those responses that affirm what is going on in, and can affect, the inner man.

Now, where does the Bible fit into this equation? Next we'll explain how God uses the Bible to speak to the inner man.

Romans 12:2 is the completion of a tremendous amount of doctrinal teaching and theology by Paul. He taught about God's wrath in chapters 1 through 3. He covered justification and imputed righteousness in chapters 3 through 5 as well as sanctification and practical righteousness in chapters 6 through 8. He explained the doctrine of election and Israel's rejection of its Messiah in chapters 9 through 11. Then in chapter 12 to the end of Romans, he instructs in practical applications of the massive body of truth in the previous chapters.

So, as seen in chapters 1 through 11, because all things have been created for and are to be done for Christ's glory (11:36), we are to live a sacrificial life to Christ (12:1). Paul does not leave the reader hanging concerning how to do that. Instead, Paul starts in chapter 12 at the most critical point of how to live a sanctified life by addressing the mind (i.e., the inner man, the real you). He says in verse 2, "Do not be conformed to this world, but be transformed by the renewing of your mind, that you may prove what the will of God is, that which is good and acceptable and perfect."

If we pick this verse apart a little, it will give us a better understanding of how the Bible fits into this equation. First, look at the word *conformed*. The word Paul uses here gives the sense of an outward expression. Paul is saying don't let your outward expression be conformed to that of this world. Paul knows what the Lord has already taught. He knows that out of the heart the mouth speaks (Matt. 12:34; 15:18–19; Mark 7:21; Luke 6:45). Furthermore, Paul has just taught that because of our purpose in life, to glorify God, and because of God's mercies toward us, we are to not let ourselves—mind or body—be conformed to this world.

Paul then moves on to teach that in contrast to a worldly conformation we must have transformation. We must be changed. Our outer man must manifest a change consistent with a changed nature, or essence. In other words, we must manifest on the outside that which God has made us to be on the inside. Yes, Paul has said they have been saved. Yes, all the promises, realities, and future glory are theirs. They have been justified and redeemed with a view to living for God's glory. Yes, all that is true, Paul says. Now live it out. Manifest on the outside what you are on the inside: a new person created by God.

But how are we to do that, exactly? We know we are not to be conformed to the world. We also know we are to be transformed, and we have been; we also know we are to manifest the truth of our transformation on the outside. But what does that look like? Where are we to start?

Paul says we are to start with the "renewing of your mind." The word for *renewing* paints the picture of the act of establishing something in a like-new, improved manner. We are to establish our "mind" in a new and improved manner. We are not to have a mind that is conformed to the world but a *better* mind, a mind that is transformed, renewed, and improved. Yet how are we to have that kind of mind? Paul has taught in the previous chapters of Romans that when one is saved by God, they have been given a new nature. They have been given a new mind capable of new thoughts. Their inner person has been redeemed. They have the Holy Spirit, and they have the Scriptures to influence their thinking (Rom. 8:2, 4–6, 9, 11, 13–14, 16, 23, 26–27; 12:2).

That is exactly where the Bible fits into the equation. It tells us how and what we ought to think. The Bible influences the mind of the new man. We have been given the Holy Spirit and the ability to understand and be influenced by the Word of God. At the same time, we must read the Word with the intent to obey it. Like an umbrella left at home during a rainstorm, the Bible will do us no good if we don't use it. In fact, the Greek verb for *be transformed* is a passive imperative, meaning we are commanded to let ourselves be transformed by the renewing of our mind. In other words, we are to pick up God's Word, read it, and let it change our thinking so that we obey it rather than disobey it. That is how our minds avoid conformation to the world, realize transformation, and experience godly manifestations of that transformation. The Bible changes our minds. In Romans 12:1 we are called to a commitment in Christ, and in verse 2 we are to maintain that commitment by the renewing of our minds.[10] Our minds are

---

10 F. E. Gaebelein et al., eds., *The Expositor's Bible Commentary: Romans through Galatians* (Grand Rapids: Zondervan, 1976), 10:128.

transformed by a commitment to letting God's Word change the way we think.

Thus, we have the mind being influenced by God and His Word, which then sends the corresponding thoughts, choices, and feelings to the outer man. The outer man, by way of the brain's chemicals, then exhibits physiological responses in keeping with a transformed mind. That is how the brain's chemicals fit into the equation. The brain, which uses chemicals, is the organic link God created between the inner man—which in this case is being influenced by Scripture—and the outer man. Since this is true, what kinds of thoughts do we want our link to intercept? Do we want conformed worldly thoughts or transformed sanctified thoughts making chemical reactions in the brain?

With that question in mind, let's look at an example. Let's say, for instance, there is a married couple named John and Sally. Sally is a housewife who suffers from intermittent but severe stomach cramps. John is the average working man who commutes to work each morning.

One morning on his way to work, John is in a car accident. He was in a line of traffic that had come to a stop. John was paying attention to the traffic flow, so he stopped just fine. However, the driver in the work truck behind him was not paying attention. In fact, the truck was still going at a decent rate of speed. The only thing that got the driver's attention was the impact with the back of John's car. That impact pushed the trunk of John's car all the way into the back seat. It also propelled John's car into the car in front of him, smashing that car's rear and crumpling the hood of John's car too.

John suffered some injuries to his knees and back, but it was nothing life threatening. So John called Sally and told her about the accident. At this point there is tension in Sally's life, but tension in and of itself isn't bad or wrong.[11] Tension can be either harnessed as a servant or heeded as a master.

The symptoms of tension the wife experiences in the outer person are an elevated heartrate, dilated pupils, and sweaty palms due to adrenalin excretion. And though she may not feel it, her liver is secreting additional glucose for fuel. So the inner man's thoughts—Sally's tension—were sent to Sally's brain, her brain provided the appropriate chemical responses, and the brain and its chemicals then triggered the corresponding physical responses.

Sally is experiencing tension, which has led to a heightened stance of alert. The inner person has affected the outer. Her body is now physiologically prepared to handle possibly dangerous circumstances.

Now there is a fork in the road. There is evidence to be observed (i.e., the accident), but how will Sally interpret that evidence? What worldview will Sally use? She has already done a preliminary interpretation of the evidence. She has concluded that this is a tension-warranting event, and that's okay. But the rest of the conclusion—what she will do with that tension—will be decided by her worldview. Is her mind conformed or transformed, and how would the scenario turn out either way? Does she misuse the tension and become full of anxiety by focusing on self and circumstances first, or does she use the tension and accomplish a task unto God's glory by focusing on Christ first? Will she respond like a worldly person or like one whose mind has been renewed by the Spirit and the Word? Let's look at both options.

---

11 Jay E. Adams, *The Christian Counselor's Manual: The Practice of Nouthetic Counseling* (Grand Rapids: Zondervan, 1973), 420.

First, what if she reacts in a self-centered, materialistic way? What if she first thinks about what this accident means to their financial status? What if her first concern is whether John can still work? What might happen to her touchy stomach if she misuses the tension? We could see the inner person affecting the outer in that Sally might encourage or exacerbate physiological problems that arise out of her unbiblical thinking. Her stomach cramps could be triggered or get worse. Those cramps could put her down in bed, making her a liability to her husband instead of a help. What if her wrong thinking exacerbates her cramps enough to put her in the hospital? Now there are two people down. Being in the hospital would add more question to their financial stability. That could lead to more anxiety on Sally's part, and that could lead to worse cramps. It's a vicious circle. Meanwhile, poor John is still on the side of the road! Sally has failed at being a help to him but succeeded in being a hindrance. Worst of all, Sally, in this instance, is displeasing the Lord. She has not had her thinking renewed by His Word. She has a wrong worldview. She is heeding her tension as a master. She is having sinful responses.

But what if Sally chooses the other side of the fork in the road? How might she harness the tension as a servant rather than heed it as a master? She would do that by having a biblical worldview—by renewing her mind. She could start by being thankful to the Lord that it's not any worse and for the opportunity for sanctification in the circumstances the Lord has sovereignly brought about. After all, John is still alive and able to call her on the phone. If she uses the tension properly, she would eliminate physiological problems that arise out of unbiblical thinking. She could use the extra energy to be helpful to John instead of being an anxious liability. Best of all, she would be pleasing to the Lord because she has heeded His Word.

At this time there ought to be another clarification. We are not saying all anxiety is wrong. Anxiety is fear, and there are two kinds of fear—godly and ungodly. An example of godly fear would be the concern for another's well-being, not because of what it means to you but because of what it means to them. That's caring about important things for the right reasons, and it is accompanied by trust in God's sovereignty. Another instance of godly fear is the fear of God. In fact, Deuteronomy 13:4 commands us to fear God.

So, not all anxiety is wrong, but anxiety that stops you from obeying God is wrong. That kind of anxiety is sinful. It is ungodly fear. That kind of anxiety worries about mere possibilities. That's the wrong worldview. It's self-centered materialistic thinking that acts as if God is not sovereign. It refuses to submit to His sovereignty.

Another instance of ungodly fear, or the wrong kind of anxiety we are considering, is that which fails to focus on God and trust Him. That kind of anxiety flows out of the example above and views the circumstances first, with God being a distant second. That kind of anxiety, then, has a distorted view of both. That kind of anxiety has the wrong filter for a worldview. It looks at the circumstances, and they look overwhelming and gigantic. And it's no wonder because it is a distorted view of the circumstances. It is not viewing them through a biblical filter to have a right perspective on God first and then the circumstances second. That is a little-God, big-problem worldview.

Those would be the right and wrong kinds of anxiety, or fear. Thus, God actually commands us to have, yet not have, anxiety. The difference is the kind of anxiety. It is the difference between the object of anxiety and the response to the object. There is a wrong and a right kind of anxiety, and God commands us to not have the wrong kind.

So that we might better understand what God means when He is talking about the wrong kind of anxiety and how we ought to respond to it, let's take a closer look at His Word. In Philippians 4:6 Paul says, "Be anxious for nothing, but in everything by prayer and supplication with thanksgiving let your requests be made known to God."

A few observations can be made of Paul's statement. First, the Greek word for "anxious" Paul uses gives the sense of fretfulness or undue concern.[12] He is telling us to not be in a state of fret or to have undue concern over what is happening or what might happen in life. Next, the verb for "be anxious" is a present-tense, imperative-mood verb. Thus, Paul is commanding the reader to continually practice something. He is saying that we need to be continually in a non-anxious state. We are to keep refraining from fretfulness and undue concern. We are to "be anxious for nothing."

Paul is commanding us to not be anxious because it indicates a lack of trust in God's wisdom and sovereignty. Being anxious despite God's Word and His indwelling Spirit demonstrates a materialistic worldview. It views the circumstances or even the possible circumstances before God, which distorts both. It is practical atheism. One might have mental assent to the truth, but if they deny the truth with their actions, they prove that it was only knowledge of the truth, not conviction of the truth. They act no better than an atheist and lack real trust in the Lord.

---

12 F. E. Gaebelein et al., eds., *The Expositor's Bible Commentary: Ephesians through Philemon* (Grand Rapids: Zondervan, 1981), 11:151.

So what are we to do when tempted to be anxious? Paul says instead of being anxious, we are to go to the Lord "in everything." If we continue reading in verse 6, we will see how to do this. Paul says we are to go to the Lord "by prayer." Prayer is worshiping God. Prayer is saying that you are incapable but He is capable. That is trusting God. That is a right worldview. Anxiety comes from the desire to control reality all the while knowing that ultimate control is not possible. We want to make something happen or not happen but realize inside that we ultimately do not have the power to make our wishes come about. Thus, we become anxious because our will may not be done. That is failure to trust God. It's pride and an unbiblical worldview. However, prayer is the exact opposite. Unlike anxiety, prayer is reverent. Unlike anxiety, prayer is humble. Unlike anxiety, prayer demonstrates a trust in God, which implies submission to His will. A person who is anxious is not submitting to the Lord's will, nor is he trusting Him.

Next, Paul says that while going to God in prayer or having a worshipful attitude, we are to also bring our "supplication." A supplication is an urgent request or plea. Paul is telling us that instead of letting your urgent request or plea turn into anxiousness we ought to bring it to the Lord in prayer. We are to make it known to God. And it's not that God is ignorant of our needs but that this is the gracious way He has ordained for us to communicate with Him. He allows and enables us to come to Him making our requests known. The God of the universe actually invites us to come and talk to Him!

Furthermore, Paul says, we are not to bring our requests to the Lord any old way. We are to bring it "with thanksgiving." Thanksgiving should accompany all Christian prayer as we acknowledge that whatever outcome the Lord brings is for our good and His glory (Rom. 8:28–29). Also, we ought to be thankful for His graciousness and mercy toward us in the past.[1]

Notice that Paul then says, "Let your requests be made known." The verb for "let be made known" is again an imperative-mood, present-tense verb. Paul is commanding us to habitually practice making our requests to God. Some people claim that we are to go to God once with our requests and leave the matter alone. They say to do otherwise shows lack of trust in the Lord. However, Paul is saying the opposite. We are to keep on going to the Lord in prayer with our requests. We are to habitually practice not being anxious and habitually practice going to the Lord in prayer. Contrary to what some say, continually going to the Lord in prayer over a matter demonstrates a trust in Him. A heart that desires to obey God's Word does so because it trusts what that Word says.

As the temptation for anxiety arises, our prayer life should rise to meet and defeat it. We are to practice replacing anxiety with persistent prayer. God commands us to keep being anxiety free. He also commands us to keep coming to Him in prayer "in everything" because He alone is sovereign over all, including what is tempting us to be anxious. D. A. Carson summed this truth up nicely when he said, "The way to be anxious about nothing is to be prayerful about everything."[2]

So we are to go to God in prayer about the entirety, the full extent, of the situation. And we are to do it because He cares for us. But where does it say that? We can look to the next verse for the answer.

---

[1] Gaebelein et al., 11:152.
[2] D. A. Carson, *Basics for Believers: An Exposition of Philippians* (Grand Rapids: Baker, 1996), 112.

In Philippians 4:7, God makes a promise to those who obediently replace anxiety with thankful prayer. He says you will have "the peace of God." God offers inner peace to those who trust Him in difficult and even dire circumstances. God promises peace to those who are His and who seek Him when in need. A God who does not care does not give peace. However, because God does care, He gives peace amid trials.

Then Paul goes on to qualify the kind of peace promised in verse 7. He says it's a peace that keeps surpassing "all comprehension." This is a supernatural peace that doesn't simply suffice; no, it *surpasses* all human comprehension. This peace God promises is superior. It surpasses and is better than the difficult circumstances.

Next, Paul tells us what this peace does. He goes on to give the function of the peace promised in verse 7. He says that this supernatural peace is a sentry to "guard your hearts" (i.e., minds). A guard had two functions: he kept things in that should stay in, and he kept things out that should stay out. And that is exactly what happens when the Spirit guards our hearts.

To guard the heart is to guard the will. It is to make sure our will matches God's will. To guard the heart is to also guard the seat of emotions. It is to make sure our emotions match His. To guard the heart is to also guard our reason. It is to make sure our reason is conformed to His. It is also to guard the conscience between right and wrong. It is to keep the heart from that which should stay out: anxiety and despair. To guard the heart is to keep watch over it. It is to detain and confine our thoughts to dwell on what is right and true.

So what is right and true? On what will our thoughts be dwelling? Paul tells us in verse 8. He says everything that is right and true, all your guarded thoughts, will be pointed back to "Christ Jesus" (v. 7). Think about it. There is no one else in the history of mankind who encompasses the attributes of verse 8 more than Christ. Jesus is the truest—most consistent with fact. He is the most honorable—the most sacred. He is the ultimate example and standard of right—in harmony with the Father's standard. He is the most morally pure, the supreme example of loveliness, of kindness and graciousness. He lays rightful claim to the highest repute, is held in the highest regard. He is the Author and standard of moral excellence, the worthiest of praise. Combat the temptation to be anxious with prayer to the Author of peace, and He will help you keep your thoughts, guard your thoughts, and watch over your thoughts so that they focus on Him. God promises a supernatural peace that will confine our thoughts so they will dwell "in Christ Jesus," not on the circumstances.

This is not to say that the Christian should fail to act or to plan in difficult circumstances. Circumstances may not change just because we have prayed. When faced with the temptation to be anxious, Christians ought to act and plan in a mindset that is bathed in prayer. The peace and guarded heart Paul is talking about are a supernatural peace and guarded heart in the midst of the circumstances. This is Romans 12:2 coming to pass. This is "the renewing of your mind."

Now, back to the car accident scenario. If the wife whose husband called about an accident responds in this way, there will be, as Paul says, "the peace of God" amid the trial. The cure for anxiety and for unbiblical thinking is to trust God and ask Him to help us change our mind, our focus. We are to change our focus from our circumstances to the Savior. Unbiblical thinking, a wrong worldview that dwells on the circumstances, does have its consequences. How we think, how we interpret life, can have physiological and theological consequences, and those consequences have been determined by God. The Lord has ordained that we can become sick because of wrong thinking. We need to ask ourselves if we are sick because of wrong thinking.

The last example in this category is, sadly, a particularly common example in many homes across the country. It is sickness or injury suffered by one person due to the unbiblical attitudes of another. This is physical and sexual abuse in the home, and the number of victims is staggering. Michael Petit, president of Every Child Matters, a children's advocacy organization, says that "over the past 10 years, more than 20,000 American children are believed to have been killed in their own homes by family members. That is nearly four times the number of US soldiers killed in Iraq and Afghanistan."[3]

That's not all. The National Center for Injury Prevention and Control states some of our national statistics for domestic violence, and the numbers are heartbreaking. They report that one in three women and one in four men have experienced physical violence by an intimate partner.[4]

Think of the people you know. Take a look around you in the workplace, in the movie theater, and even in the church pew. Most likely 33 percent of women you see and 25 percent of men have suffered some kind of domestic abuse. These are real people suffering real abuse, and as we know, abuse can lead to murder or suicide. There are some of those

---
3 Michael Petit, "Why child abuse is so acute in the US," *BBC News*, October 11, 2011, https://www.bbc.com/news/magazine-15193530.
4 Michele C. Black et al., "National Intimate Partner and Sexual Violence Survey: 2010 Survey Report," National Center for Injury Prevention and Control, published November 2011, https://www.cdc.gov/violenceprevention/pdf/nisvs_report2010-a.pdf.

statistics too. The National Coalition Against Domestic Violence (NCADV) states that "72% of all murder-suicides involve an intimate partner; 94% of the victims of these murder suicides are female," and that "a study of intimate partner homicides found that 20% of victims were not the intimate partners themselves, but family members, friends, neighbors, persons who intervened, law enforcement responders, or bystanders."[5]

So much for the idea of "what we do in our own bedroom or in our own home is none of anyone's business." There are consequences to our sin, and sometimes (about 20 percent of the time according to this statistic) someone who isn't directly involved with the abuse suffers those consequences. They pay for another's sin with their life.

Physical and sexual abuse in the home can have many devastating effects on the victim. And this says nothing of nursing home abuse, homicidal poisoning, or workplace violence. In the heat of the moment you have husbands harming wives, wives hurting husbands, children suffering injury (even death), good Samaritans getting physically wrecked, and first responders paying the ultimate price. People, due to the sin of another, can become sick, injured, or even killed because of unbiblical thoughts and attitudes.

Sin and its results can be quite horrific. If we were to end here, we could feel quite hopeless. Therefore, it's at this point that we will begin to consider some benefits of being sick.

---

5 "National Statistics," NCADV, accessed December 1, 2020, https://ncadv.org/statistics.

3

Why Beneficial Sickness Might Sound Odd

People talk about the benefits of being healthy all the time, but they rarely talk about the advantages of being sick. Usually, when someone gets sick, the first thought, the goal, is to get back to health quickly. We suggest, however, that is the wrong mindset. It may sound antithetical to one's thinking to believe that sickness can actually be beneficial, but it can. In fact, the Bible gives us several benefits to being sick.

Of course, having good stewardship of the health God gave us is not wrong. But the typical view of sickness is unbiblical. At least three reasons come to mind why the idea of beneficial sickness might sound so odd to us.

But before we examine how sickness can be beneficial, let's briefly examine why we may not have thought about it that way. Below we will look at three reasons why the concept of beneficial sickness may sound odd so we can examine ourselves in the light of Scripture in order to view God and our sickness rightly.

Because We Might Not Be Biblically Minded

First, beneficial sickness may sound odd because we are not, by nature, biblically minded. People fail to be biblically minded when they neglect to study the Scriptures daily with the intent to obey. If one does not know God or what He is like as revealed in His Word, and if one does not know what God says in His Word, then he will not know how to think like Him (see Col. 3:15–17).[6]

Furthermore, it is not enough to simply skim over the Word or to read it in a hurried way. There is a difference between reading Scripture and feeding on Scripture. Simply reading Scripture out of ritualistic function can easily be more of a chore to complete to move on to the next task. Feeding on Scripture, on the other hand, is taking your time to understand it and apply it, which is vital to all Christians. In fact, John MacArthur says, "Continual feeding on the truths of Scripture is essential to the spiritual health of all Christians."[7]

Because the difference is critical to our thinking, let's make a comparison of the two by way of illustration. When we spend time with our spouse, do we watch the clock? Do we mentally check off a box so we can move on to the next task?

---

[6] In Col 3:15, we are commanded to let the peace of Christ rule our hearts. The only way for that to happen is to salvifically know Christ. The only source of revelation about Christ is Scripture (v. 16), which we are commanded to have dwell, or live, richly in our hearts and minds. The result (i.e., knowing Christ and living richly in His Word) is that we will think and live like Him. Verse 16 gives us the results of that life: wisdom. We will begin to teach, admonish, and counsel one another (v. 16). We will have the result of joyful worship, which will manifest itself in psalms, hymns, spiritual songs, and singing with gratitude to God (v. 16). Moreover, verse 17 teaches us that we will act consistently with who God is and what He does. We will thankfully do all in word and deed as Christ's representatives (i.e., "in the name of the Lord Jesus").

[7] John MacArthur, *1 & 2 Timothy: Encouragement for Church Leaders* (Nashville: Nelson, 2007), 45.

Do we pay little attention to what they say, or do we study what they say? Do we spend quality time with them? Do we want to be with them? Is the effort given to know them better?

If not, why not? Might we suggest, in this instance, that there is a lack of love in the heart for God and others. Someone might argue, "But I don't have time for all that!" First Corinthians 13:4 says, "Love is patient." One may object, "But my spouse is cold toward me" or "Their concerns seem trivial." Paul answers, "Love is kind . . . and is not arrogant." Someone might protest, "But I rarely get the attention and affection I want." Paul responds, "Love . . . is not jealous." Yet someone might still disagree, "But you don't know what he or she is like. They need me to put them in their place!" But Paul asserts, "[Love] does not act unbecomingly; it does not seek its own, is not provoked, does not take into account a wrong suffered, does not rejoice in unrighteousness, but rejoices with the truth; bears all things, believes all things, hopes all things, endures all things" (1 Cor. 13:5–7).

Are we not glad that God doesn't treat us that way? What if God said, "I don't have time for you"? What if God said, "But you're cold toward Me"? What if God said, "I rarely if ever receive the attention and affection from you I deserve"? What if God just couldn't find a way to cover your sin? What's more, if God were to make any of these claims against us, He would be right! Yet He lavishes us with love. That is truly amazing grace toward us. In view of all this, aren't we willing to spend some time with God by feeding on His Word?

The Bible is God's self-revelation. It is His divinely inspired love letter on how to know Him and avoid His wrath. Thus it logically follows that if we don't know God or read the Bible, then we won't know what He has revealed about Himself. We will not be training in righteous thinking or action, nor will we know how God thinks or acts—and so we won't be able to imitate Him. In this case, we will not think or act like God, especially when we become sick. We need to feed on Scripture daily to be biblically minded.

With the above being said, in 1 Corinthians 2:14–16 Paul tells us that the believer, in contrast to the natural man, has been given the ability to discern divine truth through the empowering Holy Spirit and the illuminating Word. However, Scripture will be of no benefit to us unless we read it with the intent to obey it through the empowering Spirit. To be biblically minded, we need the Word *and* the Spirit. Speaking to this truth, Michael Lawrence says, "We can't deduct who God is from what we're like. God is spirit and God is holy. He is our Creator and our Lord. That means that knowledge of God will demand of us reverence, obedience, and worship. It also means that such knowledge will have to be given to us. We won't be able to discover it on our own. If we are to know God, God must reveal himself. And the place he has revealed himself is through the inspired revelation of Scripture."[1]

If we do not avail ourselves to what God has given us in His Word, we cannot be surprised, upset, or disappointed when we fail to think and act like Him during trials. We have been given His Spirit and the Scriptures. We must use our Holy Spirit-empowered minds to read and employ the Scriptures daily.

---

[1] Michael Lawrence, *Biblical Theology in the Life of the Church: A Guide for Ministry* (Wheaton, IL: Crossway, 2010), 101.

Because Our Theology Might Be Wrong

Second, beneficial sickness may sound odd to us because of bad theology. The truth of God's sovereignty over our sickness and all its aspects can initially be hard to understand. This can be the case for a variety of reasons. For example, we may have believed the prosperity gospel. The prosperity gospel, or health and wealth teaching, is bad theology. The prosperity gospel teaches that God wants us to be happy, healthy, and wealthy. That kind of teaching is easy to believe and desire because it speaks to everything the flesh already wants. It focuses on comfort here and now. It's a gospel of immediate gratification, and it distorts the true gospel and true Christianity. In the prosperity gospel's plan, we can have heaven now! We can have no pain, no sickness, and plenty of wealth.

The prosperity gospel tells us that all we need to do to unlock health and wealth in our lives is believe enough and it will happen. So then it's the power of our belief that heals us, not God's sovereign and providential power, should He choose to heal. Our belief that we will get well, our faith in our forthcoming health, becomes the object of our highest hope instead of unbroken, eternal fellowship with God in heaven. Speaking to the danger and error associated with such earthbound teaching and affections, John MacArthur says:

> We live in an era of immediate gratification.... We prefer instant gratification, and we all too willingly sacrifice the future on the altar of the immediate.
>
> Again, Christians are not exempt from this tendency. Rather than setting their affections on things above, many tend to become attached to the things of this

earth. . . . Worse, certain high-profile media ministries, preaching a prosperity gospel, give multitudes the disastrous impression that this is what Christianity is all about. They promise people that Jesus wants them healthy, wealthy, and successful. Such teaching is extremely popular because it caters to the spirit of the age—and the desire to have everything in this life, right now.[2]

Bad theology, such as the prosperity gospel, fails to seek the things above (Col. 3:1–2). Instead, it seeks the things below, on the earth.

Speaking about seeking things on the earth, there is another disastrous part to the prosperity gospel. And this part revolves around money: the sick or injured person needs to send their money to the prosperity teacher. Don't forget that part. Even though in the teacher's scheme it is said to be the power of the sick person's faith that heals, the prosperity teacher's need for the sick person's money is even more powerful. So if someone doesn't send the money, then the teacher cannot help them. And they say they cannot help because the person lacks the faith to be healed as evidenced by the lack of their personal finances pledged to the "healer." In the end, the sick person has an empty promise of health at best and a distorted view of God at worst. Meanwhile, the prosperity teacher has the realization of newfound wealth. Then to add insult to injury, when the sick or crippled person fails to get better, the blame is placed on that person for their lack of faith. So now the scam victim is left sick, broke, and blaming themselves for a faith that is too weak to heal. It's a tragedy on many levels. Bad theology gets us there and much worse.

---

[2] John MacArthur Jr., *The Glory of Heaven: The Truth About Heaven, Angels, and Eternal Life* (Wheaton, IL: Crossway, 1998), 46–47.

Because We Might Have the Wrong Focus

Third, beneficial sickness may sound odd to us because of bad focus. If our worldview is self-focused rather than God-focused, then the idea of beneficial sickness will seem foreign and even silly to us. A self-focused worldview has a high view of self and a low view of God. Someone with a self-focused worldview looks at the world and asks, "What does this mean to me?" They read Scripture and first ask, "What does this mean to me?" A worldview turned inward inevitably promotes the sin of pride. God hates pride (Prov. 6:16–19; 8:13). Pride blinds the eyes to one's own sin and God's glory and eliminates teachability. The lack of teachability renders one's mind foolish and fallacious. A fool despises instruction (Prov. 1:7; 18:2). The end of a fool is not knowledge and understanding but beatings and judgment (Prov. 10:13; 16:5; 19:29; 26:3). A self-focused worldview believes all is from me, for me, to me, and by me.[3] *I deserve all good things, so why am I sick?*

In contrast, a God-focused worldview has a high view of God and a low view of self. A person with a God-focused worldview looks at the world and asks, "How can I use this world and all that is in it to glorify God?" They read Scripture and ask, "What is this teaching me about God?" and then, "How do I apply what I just read in my life?" A God-focused worldview promotes humility because it is always looking at God. That is genuine humility manifested through teachability.

It is well worth noting that God loves genuine humility so much that He promises the humble will inherit the kingdom

---

3 Stuart Scott, *From Pride to Humility: A Biblical Perspective* (Bemidji, MI: Focus, 2002), 12.

of heaven (Matt. 5:3). The humble are regarded by God (Ps. 138:6; Isa. 66:2), heard by God (Ps. 9:12; 10:17), blessed by God (Matt. 5:3), and gain knowledge through the proper fear of God (Prov. 1:7). A person with a God-focused worldview is a teachable person (Col. 3:16). The end of a God-focused worldview is exaltation by God (James 4:10; 1 Peter 5:6, 10). A God-centered worldview says all is from God, by God, and to God's glory.[4] A Christian with a God-centered worldview trusts God in all circumstances, even when sick or dying (Rom. 8:28–29; 1 Cor. 10:13; James 1:2–4; Phil. 4:6–8). A God-centered worldview believes in this way: Since I deserve worse than my current circumstances, since God is for me, and since He can be trusted, I need to learn how to use my suffering to His glory.

Pastor John MacArthur, writing about the need to avoid self-centered theology, and the difference between a Christ-centered and man-centered worldview and their implications says:

> Many forces hinder our understanding of this basic truth: the goal of every Christian's life is to become more like Christ. Humanistic psychology is one such force. It teaches that man exists for his own satisfaction—he must have all his perceived needs and desires met to be happy. As a result, in many churches spiritual growth is often equated with ironing out life's problems and finding personal fulfillment.
>
> That kind of mentality ultimately leads to a man–centered theology, which is diametrically opposed to what the Bible teaches. The goal of salvation and sanctification is that we be conformed to the image of Christ (Rom. 8:29). It's been well said that faith looks out instead of in,

---

[4] Scott, 25.

and the whole of life falls into line. The more you know Christ and focus on Him, the more the Spirit will make you like Him. But the more you focus on yourself, the more distracted you will be from the proper path.[5]

Now that a God-centered worldview has been set forth, let's next look at some of the benefits of being sick.

---

[5] John MacArthur, *Truth for Today: A Daily Touch of God's Grace* (Nashville: J. Countryman, 2001), 159.

4

Six Benefits of Sickness

So now that we have made it past the odd concept of sickness being a potential benefit, let's dig a bit deeper into some specific ways that God's Word outlines the eternal value of sickness in our lives. While I propose six benefits here, I am confident my readers have experienced other benefits I did not cover.

God's Glory

Since God is foremost about bringing glory to Himself (1 Chr. 16:28–29; Ps. 22:23; Isa. 42:8, 12; John 8:50; Rom. 11:36; Phil. 2:11; 1 Peter 4:11; Rev. 5:13), it follows that the best benefit of sickness with which to start is that of bringing God glory through our sickness. In other words, we tend to think of sickness as a bad thing or simply something to suffer through, but God uses sickness and death to bring glory to Himself, and that's a good thing. Therefore, we ought to realize this benefit and work with God to bring Him glory through our sickness. To this end we will briefly consider three examples:

Jesus's healing of the official's son, Jesus's healing of a blind man, and Jesus's raising of a dead man.

The first example is in John 4:43–54. It is there that Jesus heals an official's son who was sick and near death. At this time Jesus was two days removed from His cross-cultural evangelism in Samaria (vv. 39–42). Now He arrives in Galilee, which continued His trip from Judea (vv. 3, 43). In Samaria Jesus was honored as Messiah (v. 42). However, in Galilee He found no such honor (v. 44). The Galileans only received Him in order to satisfy their curiosity in His miracles (v. 45, 48).

Among those who were curious about Jesus's miracles was a royal official whose son was mortally ill. The official's son, though, was not with him in Galilee. He was at home in Capernaum (v. 46). When the official heard that Jesus was in the area, he went to see Him to request healing for his son (v. 47). The tense of the verb for "requesting" tells us that he was constantly requesting of Jesus. He was imploring Jesus to heal his son. This man was desperate for Jesus to heal his son of sickness, but it was desperation motivated only by Jesus's miracles, not in who He was. The official disregarded who Jesus was through his unbelief and simply wanted a miracle. He wanted the gift but not so much the Giver. So Jesus chided him, and others, for that kind of thinking (v. 48).

Nevertheless, Jesus chose to be gracious to the official. He told the man, "Go your way; your son lives" (v. 50). It was at this time that Jesus healed the official's son (v. 53). At the same time, Jesus created a dilemma of faith for the unbelieving official. Jesus had performed no observable, verifiable miracle in the official's presence. But observable and verifiable are exactly what the official wanted to see (v. 48). He also wanted his son to be made well, and he knew about Jesus's ability to heal. So, on the one hand, if the father refused to return to Capernaum without Jesus, he would show that he did not believe Jesus's word and risk losing any benefit because of his distrust. On the other hand, if he obeyed Jesus's command to go back home, he would be returning with no assurance, no observable evidence, that his son would be made well.

What would the father do? The father believed Jesus's word and set out for home (v. 50). He "learned faith by the compulsion of necessity."[6] The father's reaction was to believe Jesus's words without a sign. The result was that God was glorified.

Then on his way home he not only received word that his son was indeed made well but learned it was at the exact time Jesus had said, "Your son lives" (vv. 51–53). Next came the reaction: "he himself believed, and his whole household" (v. 53). Again, the result was that God was glorified. The official went from not believing Jesus's word to believing it, and it all came about because of God's graciousness toward him. God is glorified when one believes the word of Christ.

Our second example is in John 9:1–38 where Jesus heals a man who was born blind. John 9:1–3 says, "As [Jesus] passed by, He saw a man blind from birth. And His disciples asked Him, saying, 'Rabbi, who sinned, this man or his parents, that he should be born blind?' Jesus answered, 'It was neither that this man sinned, nor his parents; but it was in order that the works of God might be displayed in him.'"

This was a time of high intensity hatred against Jesus. The murmuring against Him in chapters 5 and 6 has become outright viciousness. The Jews had had enough of Jesus's

---

6 F. E. Gaebelein et al., eds. *The Expositor's Bible Commentary: John and Acts* (Grand Rapids: Zondervan, 1981), 9:60.

Messianic claims and attempted to kill Him. They did not believe His claim of who He was. He had broken their traditions, challenged their authority, and drew their coveted crowds to Himself through His miracles. For that, the Jews hated Him. However, it was the claim of divinity that most infuriated them (8:58–59). It was for that claim that they tried to stone Him to death, but they were unable to because He went out through the midst of them. It was not yet God's time for Him to die, so Jesus still lived. He escaped the murder attempt on His life.

After Jesus escaped the Jews' murderous efforts, He and His disciples were walking through Jerusalem. In God's timing, "as He passed by, He saw a man blind from birth" (9:1). His disciples saw the man, too, but erroneously deduced that the man's condition was due to sin on his or his parents' part (v. 2). Jesus corrected their wrong thinking and said that the man was born blind not because of sin but "in order that the works of God might be displayed in him" (v. 3). This man's infirmity was ordained by God so that God could use him as a vehicle to glorify Himself through His Son. God is sovereign over the healing as well as the sickness, and it was all for His glory.

Jesus began to heal the blind man and used the same substance He used to create man in the first place (Gen. 2:7)—dust from the ground that He mixed with spittle (v. 6). Then He applied the clay to the man's eyes and told him, "Go, wash in the pool of Siloam" (v. 7). As with the official in the first example, this man found himself at a fork in the road. He could either disbelieve Jesus's word because there was no visible evidence, or he could believe Jesus's word.

What was the man's reaction? Also similar to the official in the first example, the man believed Jesus, trusting in His word. The evidence of that belief is that did exactly what he was told (v. 7). This man, blind from birth, chose to believe something completely unheard of in the history of mankind: that words and clay could create new eyes. And like the official, he only believed it possible after a working of God's grace toward him (v. 6). Jesus acted on him first, and then the man believed His word, which led to his healing.

But this is not the end of the story. After his neighbors' disbelief, a thorough but failed grilling from the Pharisees, his parents' failure to vouch for him, and being put out of the synagogue (vv. 8–34), Jesus met up with him once more. The man was about to be transferred into God's kingdom. Jesus asked him, "Do you believe in the Son of Man?" (v. 35). The blind man, having never seen Jesus, asked who the Messiah—the Son of Man—was so he may believe (v. 36). Then, in verse 37, Jesus plainly tells him that he is talking with the Messiah. What was the man's reaction? The man believed Jesus and worshiped Him (v. 38). Because of God's initial graciousness in this man's life, the man believed and gained both physical and spiritual sight. What were the results? Jesus was worshiped, and the Father was glorified.

Our last example is in John 11:17–45. Here Jesus raised a dead man named Lazarus from the grave. John 11–12:50 marks a transition point in Jesus's life. He was at the end of His public ministry. Up until now, the Jews had squandered their opportunity with their Messiah. Instead of committing to Him, they wanted to kill Him. Now Jesus moves more into seclusion. He knows He is not far from His ordained crucifixion. So He begins to minister more exclusively to His disciples and the ones who loved Him.

During this time in Jesus's life and ministry, He was told that His friend Lazarus was deathly ill (vv. 1–3). Jesus assured the messengers of Lazarus's sisters that God's divine purpose in the illness that would result in death was to glorify God (v. 4). Not long after this, Lazarus dies (vv. 11–14).

Then as Jesus tells His disciples that Lazarus has died, He tells them why He allowed the death to happen. He said the purpose in Lazarus's death was so that they would believe in Him (v. 15). What else could this mean except that Jesus was going to raise Lazarus in front of the disciples and others in order to strengthen their faith in Him as Messiah? Jesus knew His disciples and loved ones were going to need more faith in the face of growing opposition toward Him, so He ordains an opportunity to accomplish that. By God's divine plan Lazarus would die, but he would also be raised in the sight of many.

Four days after Lazarus's death, Jesus was approaching his tomb after having journeyed from the place He had been (v. 17). The Jews did not embalm dead bodies. Instead, they wrapped them up tight, put many pounds of spices on top of the body to lessen the smell of decay, and placed them in the tomb on the same day.[7] However, by this time, Lazarus's body had been in the tomb four days. The decomposition of his body was well underway. There was no doubt that Lazarus was dead.

As Jesus approaches Lazarus's tomb, Martha went out to meet Him (v. 20). In a statement of trust, Martha told Him, "Lord, if You had been here, my brother would not have died" (v. 21). Martha was mourning her brother's death. At the same time, she knew Jesus was the Messiah. She knew that He could bring something good out of this sad event (v. 22).

---

7 *The Lexham Bible Dictionary*, J. D. Barry et al., eds., (Bellingham, WA: Lexham, 2016), s.vv. "seal" "tomb."

Having compassion for one of His loved ones and knowing the plan of God, Jesus then mercifully informs Martha, "Your brother shall rise again" (v. 23). Martha responds to Jesus's statement with an abstract view of resurrection (v. 24). She knows the resurrection will happen on the last day, but her brother is dead today, and naturally, she wants him back today. So Jesus answers Martha and clears up her confusion. He moves her from her abstract thinking of a future resurrection to the concrete thinking of trust in the Person of the resurrection by pointing her to Himself. Jesus is the only One who can raise the dead (v. 25). He then asks her, "Do you believe this?" (v. 26). What was Martha's reaction? In verse 27 she says, "Yes, Lord; I have believed that You are the Christ, the Son of God, even He who comes into the world." Moreover, she believed Him, like in the other examples, without observable evidence. After all, her brother was still dead four days at this point.

As the narrative continues, in a preview of the power of the final resurrection, Jesus raises Lazarus from the dead in front of many people (vv. 30–44). What was the reaction to this miracle? Verse 45 tells us that many of the Jews who had witnessed the resurrection believed in Him. The Jews had heard His words, seen His grief for His friend, heard His prayer of thanks to the Father, heard His command to the dead, witnessed His power over death, and believed in Him.

What were the results of this miracle? God was glorified. The miracle, as well as the death that made it necessary, identified Jesus as the Messiah, and many believed in Him. Believing in the Son glorifies the Father who sent Him.

It's a given that these examples are extreme. The normative process is that people experience sickness, dysfunction, and death without miraculous intervention. Yet the extreme nature of these examples in no way diminishes the fact that God uses sickness and death to glorify Himself. In fact, it accomplishes the complete opposite. The extreme nature of these examples glorifies God. If He can glorify Himself with Lazarus who died and a man who cannot see, He can glorify Himself in someone who has not yet died and who can see!

In each of the examples above we can observe that God had a primary purpose for the illness or deformity. And that primary purpose was to bring glory to Himself. Secondary to that and through an expression of His mercy, God healed. God is primarily for His glory, secondarily for the healing of people.

Now, there are some implications to these primary and secondary purposes. This means that Christ's primary purpose for healing each person was not better health for them but more glory for God. We need to get this concept right. God's primary purpose in one's life is not better health. God's primary purpose is His own glorification. His secondary purpose is the healing through which He is glorified. God's glory is what God is about. The healings are always secondary and incidental.

Was God merciful and gracious in the healings in our examples? Yes! The healings were an expression of that. God is kind. But God is also, and primarily, for His own glory.

Although this concept comes as a surprise to our self-centered culture and mentality, it really should not. It might help us fight the wrong mindset if we consider that God operates this way concerning a much more important reality. He emphasizes His glory first even in our salvation. And our salvation was due to God's kindness. In Ephesians 1:4–6, we see that God is immensely kind. Paul says "He chose us . . .

according to the kind intention of His will." Then Paul gives the main purpose in God's kind intentions. He says that God chose some for salvation "to the praise of the glory of His grace" (v. 6). God's primary purpose in saving His people was to bring Himself praise and glory through the demonstration of His grace toward the guilty. God doesn't save people because they are worthy. He saves people because He wants to glorify Himself through saving the unworthy. The kindness of God is that He is willing to save anyone at all. God's main purpose in that saving is His glory. God's secondary purpose in salvation is our saving.

Likewise, God doesn't heal people because they are worthy. He heals people as a means of glorifying Himself. Everything God does has at its core the motive of His glory (Isa. 42:8; Rom. 11:36). He saves those whom He chooses, to bring Himself glory, and He heals those whom He chooses, to bring Himself glory.[8] Since God's primary purpose is His own glory, how do we come to the conclusion that His primary purpose is our health? That was not the case in any of the examples we saw earlier. God has not changed His modus operandi (Isa. 46:9–11; Mal. 3:6; James 1:17).

Did the people in these examples benefit from God's desire to glorify Himself through healing? Yes! But we have benefitted too. How exactly do we benefit? Throughout His ministry, Jesus healed both believers and unbelievers (see Matt. 8:16; 15:30; Mark 1:34). Many were healed, but only a few were saved (Matt. 7:14; 22:14). We may not be healed, but we are saved. Which one do we prefer? Either way—healed or saved—or in both cases, God will be glorified.

---

[8] While we do not see miracles in our time like Jesus performed during His time on earth, we do benefit from His mercy and grace through modern-day medicine.

Since God's primary purpose is His glory, it logically follows that His people's primary purpose ought to be the same. We need to understand this, especially when trying to understand how we are to think and act while sick. We are to think and act so as to glorify God. So, how do we achieve that?

To glorify God, we need to be a holy people (Eph. 1:4; 5:27). In fact, 1 Peter 1:16 says, "You shall be holy, for I am holy." Notice it does not say, "You shall be healthy, for I am holy." It says, "You shall be holy, for I am holy." Christians glorify God most when they act like Him by living holy lives. Belief in Christ brings God glory and makes one holy. That does not necessarily make one healthy, but that's not God's main purpose. God's glory is God's main purpose; thus, as His people, God's glory should be our primary concern—whether we see healing or not.

If God determines that sickness or deformity should linger in our life, then our primary goal should not be the eradication of the sickness or deformity but how to best glorify God in the midst of it. It is entirely possible that no doctor could successfully diagnose, treat, or cure what ails us. In fact, it may be a matter of God's glory that we aren't made well. Not everyone in the Bible was healed. For example, it was God's will that Paul left Trophimus sick in Miletus (2 Tim. 4:20). Sometimes God uses sickness to accomplish His will.

If God should choose for His own glory that we are not made well, what would most please Him? Would it be chasing all kinds of possible solutions or responding to the circumstances in all possible ways that are pleasing to Him? Moreover, does not God have a right over our bodies? Yes, of course. In fact, He has the right over our souls too (Rom. 9:14–24). The way He chooses to exercise His right over His people is His prerogative, and it is always right. He may not choose to heal us, but He has chosen to save His own. That is far better than physical healing, and it is for His glory too.

So if the primary goal or focus of our life is to get better, then we have missed the point. The main point is God's glory, not feeling better and being pain free. Granted, this can be a difficult concept to grasp, especially when suffering is deep and long lasting. But it will be a tremendous help for us to remember two truths about God. One, God is kind in His intentions toward us. Even if believers are not healed while on earth, we will be with Him in heaven. He has saved us. Because of His kindness, our eternity is sealed with Him.

Two, God does everything primarily for His own glory. It is a good thing, for many reasons, that God's primary purpose is His glory. One of those reasons is that He is always for Himself. This is most beneficial toward us because God is the most Holy One, which means He will always act according to His standard of holiness, in accordance with His holy character. Thus, if we remain in sickness, we can rest assured that a holy God is operating with holy intentions to glorify Himself through our sickness. Our sickness is not random. It's ordained by a holy God for His glory, primarily, and our benefit, secondarily, whether we are healed or not.

What do we do with all this information? How do we bring God glory during our sickness and disease? We believe Him. We trust God's goodness, His holiness. We rest in His kindness. We submit to His sovereignty. We worship Him, and we do all that by aligning our main purpose with His main purpose: His glory. If we think this way, our lives will be shaped by Him. If we act this way, our lives will glorify Him.

How do we work with God to bring Him glory through our sickness? We believe Him amid our suffering. That brings

God glory. That fulfills our purpose in life. And a God-glorifying life is the best benefit one can have. The first benefit of our sickness is that it brings God glory.

Christlikeness

The second way sickness can be beneficial is that it can make a believer more like Christ. Being more like Christ should be every believer's desire. Additionally, we should take great encouragement that God has the same desire for His people (see Lev. 11:44–45; 1 Peter 1:15–16). In fact, God wills that outcome for us to the extent that He predestined us to become conformed to the image of His Son (Rom. 8:29).

Since God and His Son are holy, being more like Christ requires holiness of us. The root idea of holiness is that of "separation" or "withdrawal." [9] We are to be separated or withdrawn from sin. Holiness is sanctification. Sanctification is the process by which an entity is brought into relationship with or attains the likeness of the holy.[10] Sanctification requires work. Yet sanctification has both a unilateral, or one-sided, and bilateral, or two-sided, aspect. The unilateral aspect of sanctification speaks to God's work, while the bilateral aspect speaks to God working in and with us. Either way, there is work.[11]

Sanctification, in the unilateral sense, means being set apart by God from sin to holiness so that we may serve Him (Ps. 4:3; 1 Cor. 6:11; 2 Cor. 6:17; 1 Thess. 5:23; Jude v. 1). This

---

9   *Eerdmans Dictionary of the Bible*, T. P. Jenney, D. N. Freedman, A. C. Myers, and A. B. Beck, eds., (Grand Rapids: Eerdmans, 2000), s.vv. "holiness," "holy."
10   *New Bible Dictionary*, K. E. Brower et al., eds., (Downers Grove, IL: InterVarsity, 1996), s.vv. "sanctification," "sanctify."
11   The scope of this work is not to explain sanctification in its fullness but to briefly examine its aspects.

aspect of sanctification is known as *positional sanctification* and is unilateral in function. Positional sanctification comes from God at the moment of our salvation (Col. 1:13–14). When a person is saved, he or she is positionally sanctified.[12] That is, they are set apart by God from their former standing with God as a reprobate unto their later standing with God as a saint. In other words, they are rescued by God from God's wrath and from residence in Satan's kingdom and moved in God's grace to Christ's kingdom. Concerning this truth, the apostle Paul says in Colossians 1:13–14, "For He delivered us from the domain of darkness, and transferred us to the kingdom of His beloved Son, in whom we have redemption, the forgiveness of sins."

In the passage above, it is clear that God delivers His people from the domain of darkness. It is also clear that God transfers His people to Christ's kingdom. Due to God's actions, the person's position has been changed from an evil position (the domain of darkness) to a holy position (the kingdom of His beloved Son). Additionally, we know Paul is talking about a positional sanctification that happens at the moment of salvation when he says, "We have redemption, the forgiveness of sins." If one is saved, it is because he has been redeemed and forgiven by God. The terms *redemption* and *forgiveness* are not identical. Redemption gives the sense of being released by virtue of payment, while forgiveness gives the sense of a pardon or a cancellation of debt.

For example, a few decades ago we used to get S&H Green Stamps when we shopped at the grocery store, and we would adhere those stamps into the little booklet. Once enough stamps were collected, you could take the filled booklets to

---

[12] There is also justification (i.e., God legally declares one righteous) and adoption (i.e., God makes us members of His family).

a store and exchange them for an item in the store. That exchange process was a redemption of the stamps. When the store clerk got the stamps, the item was released to us. Thus, the item's position had changed. It went from the possession of the clerk to our possession, and the item did nothing to effect the positional change. It was all due to the act of the redeemer.

Christ did the same thing but on a much larger and important scale. He redeemed, or paid for, His people by dying a substitutionary death on a cross for their sins. God the Father accepted Christ's payment as evidenced by Christ's physical resurrection from death (Rom. 1:4; 4:24–25; 6:9; 8:11, 34; Gal. 1:1; Col. 2:13–14).

Paul says the central focus of that redemption—what comes out of it—is "the forgiveness of sins." Because Christ redeemed us, because He paid for us, we are released, sent away, from "the domain of darkness" and transferred into His kingdom. Christ, by His substitutionary payment, changed our position from spiritual death to spiritual life. In other words, our redemption through Christ's substitutionary payment of our sin debt on the cross has made our pardon before God a reality. Because of Christ, our position before God has changed. It is in this position change that God works unilaterally.[13]

Next, sanctification is also progressive. We know that *sanctification* means being set apart from sin unto holiness. We also know *progressive* means that something is making progress or moving forward toward a desired end. In progressive sanctification the desired end is becoming holier and more pleasing to God through our trust and obedience empowered by the Holy Spirit. Concerning progressive sanctification, the

---

13 See also 1 Cor 6:11 for God's unilateral sanctification.

apostle Paul says in Philippians 2:12–13, "So then, my beloved, just as you have always obeyed, not as in my presence only, but now much more in my absence, work out your salvation with fear and trembling; for it is God who is at work in you, both to will and to work for His good pleasure."

In the passage above, the verb *work* is a present-tense imperative verb that tells us we are commanded to keep working our salvation out. Paul is not telling us to work for our salvation. He indicates that salvation is already possessed: your salvation. He is saying we are to "work out" that which is already in us—that is, we are to manifest through righteous works the spiritual reality already in us.

Paul then tells us the attitude with which we are to work out our salvation. We are to work it out "with fear and trembling," with a healthy fear of offending God and with great respect for Him. Love is not the Christian's only motivation. Fear is to motivate us as well. The believer is to keep working out the spiritual reality of their salvation. Thanks to Christ, the believer has a changed heart and a changed inner person (2 Cor. 5:17). He has been saved. So believers are to see that they live a life in accordance with the changed heart God has given them. They are to live a life of obedience unto God.

In verse 12 Paul talks about the Philippians' obedience: "just as you have always obeyed." He wants them to keep obeying, to keep being sanctified, to keep progressing in holiness. He wants them to keep working out that which God has placed into them—the desire and ability to obey. It is God who has given believers the desire to do His will, and it is God who has empowered them to do it.[14] So, work it out. Furthermore,

---

14 W. A. Grudem, *Systematic Theology: An Introduction to Biblical Doctrine* (Leicester, England; Grand Rapids: InterVarsity; Zondervan, 2004), 753.

they are to work it out with great reverence for God. With an attitude of reverence, believers are to make manifest that which God has placed in them—their salvation.

At the same time, the working out of obedience is not solely the effort of the believer. There is a significant bilateral aspect to it. Paul goes on to say, "For it is God who is at work in you." It is God, through His Holy Spirit, who empowers believers to keep working out their obedience, to keep working out that which is in them.

Here we can see man's responsibility to obey and God's empowering that actually produces the good works (see John 15:5; 1 Cor. 12:6). That is the progressive, bilateral aspect of sanctification. That is God empowering the believer to want to live out and work out a progressively sanctified life. This is God's Spirit empowering the believer to progressively become what he has already been positionally declared: sanctified, holy.

Why does God work with the believer like this? Because that is what pleases God. Paul says God works like this "both to will and to work for His good pleasure." God works with the believer like this so He will be satisfied with and glorified through the believer's life in the way He determined most pleases Him. So, God saves and empowers the believer to trust and obey Him, both of which are unilateral actions. Then the believer employs his God-given, God-empowered ability in a bilateral progressive process so that God is pleased and the believer becomes more sanctified.[15] God's purpose for us is to be sanctified positionally and progressively. One aspect is

---

15 This is not talking about Christian perfectionism, and neither is Paul. The very reality of a progressive sanctification eliminates the possibility of Christian perfection this side of the heaven. Christian perfection only comes when we are glorified (i.e., perfectly sanctified) in heaven (Rom. 8:30).

all of God, while the other involves our work through God's empowering.

How does all this connect to the second benefit of sickness? How does this make us more like Christ? When we work for God, when we obey Him, when we willingly suffer, when we trust His purposes for us, when we live a set-apart life from sin regardless of our circumstances, we are never more like Christ. In John 17:19 Jesus said, "For their sakes I sanctify Myself, that they themselves also may be sanctified in truth." Jesus, being sinless, was not talking about His progressive sanctification. He was talking about being totally set apart for the Father's will (4:34; 5:19; 6:38; 7:16; 9:4). Jesus lived a set-apart, truth-filled life to glorify the Father. He was completely dedicated to the Father's will even unto death on a cross.

While enduring sickness is not comparable to crucifixion, it is tough. It takes a lot of dying to self to be sanctified instead of sinning while sick. Yet, without qualification or reservation, Paul commands us to keep working out our salvation. Being sick does not absolve us of the responsibility to obey God. It just makes it more difficult.

However, we have the promise that God is working in us to achieve His desired ends. He does not leave us to our own measly efforts. He works in us to empower us to work out our salvation so that in the end, as well as along the way, He is pleased and we are sanctified.

Jesus suffered much in His life on earth. He was hungry, thirsty, tired, and tempted in all things yet without sin (Heb. 4:15). He was mocked, beaten, spit on, falsely accused of crime against man and God, whipped, and crucified. Yet, through all the revilement, He did not revile in return. Through suffering, He did not threaten but committed Himself to God, who judges righteously (1 Peter 2:23). Jesus set the example for us in suffering. He blazed the trail we are to follow. He was humble in His suffering (Phil. 2:5–8).

We are to imitate our Lord and walk with Him even through suffering and sickness. And Paul says we are to do it "with fear and trembling." We are to follow our Lord in humility. When we do that, when that is our attitude, we will be living progressively sanctified lives, lives set apart from sin unto God. And when that happens, we will be more like Christ.

There is another part to God's unilateral work of sanctification. This is saving the best for last. This is our ultimate hope. This is the guaranteed, definitive outcome of our salvation. It is perfected sanctification (Rom. 8:30; 2 Tim. 2:10). God, who unilaterally repositioned us from sinner to saint and who empowers us to obey Him, will also unilaterally glorify us to live with Him for eternity. We have been repositioned by Christ. We progressively live unto Christ, and one day, when we leave this earth, we will exist in perfection with Christ. This is the second benefit of sickness—Christlikeness—and its benefits extend well beyond the grave.

Realism

Realism can be defined as any form of belief that is disinclined toward speculation and rooted in fact.[16] Thus, the third way sickness can be beneficial is that it can help us realize the truth about our God-given mortality and fragility as opposed to speculating about it. Many of us, whether we realize it or not, live in speculation. We think that we will be around for a lot longer. We suppose that our health will stay

---

16 *The Oxford Dictionary of the Christian Church*, F. L. Cross and E. A. Livingstone, eds., (Oxford; New York: Oxford University Press, 2005), s.v. "realism."

pretty consistent or at least decline with age in a predictable, manageable fashion.

However, it is unforeseen sickness or injury that can literally shock us out of our speculation right into realism. Sickness can be used by God to redirect our thinking from speculation to the realization that our lives on this earth are short and fragile.

It is true that many young people think they are indestructible. They have the attitude that they can live life burning the candle at both ends. They take unnecessary risks and, in general, make foolish or willfully uninformed decisions thinking they can overcome any adversity. They are naive and foolish. They have neither lived long enough nor listened well enough to know better. They lack discernment in life.

As youths who have not experienced many consequences of living in a fallen world, they imagine they are going to live forever or at least not die for a long time to come. Rarely does a healthy young person ponder, even for a few seconds, the idea of long-term sickness or injury. Moreover, they surely do not ponder or even have the capacity to think ahead a few decades and realize how quickly life can pass by.

Now, if we think that the market on this kind of thinking is cornered by the young, we would be wrong. Adults fail to have a realistic view of life as well, even though they ought to know better. After all, they commit crimes too. Adults pursue immoral relationships. Adults fail to fear God. It is adults who indebt themselves up to their eyeballs, and it is adults who work themselves to their grave trying to pay back that debt. Even adults fail to realize their decisions can have serious consequences and that their life on earth is short. They ignore God and so live like practical atheists.

When there seems to be a lot of something, one rarely ponders what it would be like with a little of something. In fact, Proverbs 27:7 states, "A sated man loathes honey, but to a famished man any bitter thing is sweet." When there seems to be a lot of something—life, money, time, energy—less value is usually attached to each. But take one of those things away or restrict one of those things, and suddenly they become very valuable. One hundred dollars is nothing to a millionaire; to a single mom trying to make ends meet, it's a small fortune. And five minutes to a person on their deathbed will not be squandered as it might be by a healthy twenty-something.

Must we all wait until our later years before we consider how much time, effort, money, and energy we have wasted over the course of our lives? The answer is no. In fact, that would be poor stewardship of the life God has blessed us with. We must be good stewards of everything God has given us (Luke 12:35–38; 42–44). The Bible has a lot to say about the brevity of life. Some will learn about their mortality from the pages of Scripture. Others will be blessed by God to also experience what Scripture teaches about life's fragility through a long-term or debilitating sickness.

The Bible says that life is short. Thus, we ought to heed that reality so we can be better stewards of it. Sickness ordained by God, or providential sickness, can drive us to the reality of our short lives, but Scripture is what will shape our thoughts once there. Therefore, to help us think this way and to be encouraged to be better stewards of our God-given lives, we'll briefly consider two aspects of life. One, our brief lives are not under our control. Two, our lives are uncertain and transitory.

First, our lives are not under our control. It is God who is sovereign over them, not us. We could examine several passages concerning God's sovereignty over our lives. One example is found in Psalm 139:16. David says, "Thine eyes have seen my unformed substance; and in Thy book they were all written, the days that were ordained for me, when as yet there was not one of them." Before David was even conceived in his mother's womb, God had ordained the length of his life. That is an example of absolute sovereignty over man's life. Before David was even thought of, God knew when he would be born, when he would die, how he would die, and was sovereign over all of it.

Another example of God's sovereignty over our lives can be seen in Proverbs 16:9. Here Solomon says, "The mind of man plans his way, but the LORD directs his steps."[17] Not only is God sovereign over the beginning and end of our lives, He also overrules man's plans to fulfill His purposes. So, God is sovereign over the beginning of our lives, the end, and all the way through the middle.

In Psalm 39:5 David laments about the brevity of life when he writes, "Behold, Thou hast made my days as handbreadths, and my lifetime as nothing in Thy sight, surely every man at his best is a mere breath." At this time in David's life he is suffering greatly, and he thinks that the suffering is due, at least in part, to his personal sin. While David may not be sick here, there is a principle to be observed: intense suffering can cause one to consider the reality that their days are numbered. And so, David does just that. He compares his lifespan on earth to God's eternality by saying that the lifespan of man is so short it can be measured with the smallest popular measuring unit in the ancient world—a handbreadth, equal to about four inches. David's great suffering has brought the reality of his brief life front and center.

---

17 See also Gen. 50:20; 1 Kings 12:15; Ps. 119:133; Jer. 10:23; Dan. 5:23–28; 1 Cor. 3:19–20.

In Isaiah 40:6–8 Isaiah talks of man's transitory time on this earth against the backdrop of God's eternal word when he says, "All flesh is grass, and all its loveliness is like the flower of the field. The grass withers, the flower fades, when the breath of the LORD blows upon it; surely the people are grass. The grass withers, the flower fades, but the word of our God stands forever." Isaiah writes this about eighty years before Judah's Babylonian captivity. In the previous chapters, the prophet addresses Judah as if the captivity had already happened, in part because God has decreed it—so it is. The captivity will be brutal, and there will be suffering. This is punishment for Judah's continued sin against God. The affliction will cause them to groan and is intended to drive them back to their Lord. They will realize their life on this earth is like a fragile flower, here today, gone tomorrow. Their God-ordained suffering will shock them from presuming upon God to realistic thinking about their relationship with Him.

The second aspect of our life is that it is uncertain. James, the half-brother of Jesus, writes in his letter in James 4:14 about foolish planning that omits God and that people are living in speculation. They assume they will be able to carry out whatever plans they have, and fail to make allowances for unforeseen circumstances. So he rebukes such unwise thinking. He exposes the folly of such speculation when he writes, "You do not know what your life will be like tomorrow." Since they don't even know what their lives will be like tomorrow, they certainly have no clue about any further in the future.

Then James warns of life's transitory nature. He continues, "You are just a vapor that appears for a little while and then vanishes away." The Greek word for *vapor* can also be translated "mist."[18] James is saying that man's lifespan is like the mist. The mist is on the ground in the morning but gone by noon. That is the very definition of being transitory. They were trying to speculate about their business plans in the future as if they could control and accomplish whatever they wanted, but in reality they do not even control a few hours ahead. Their life on this earth was fleeting, and so is ours. Therefore, it is foolish to make plans without the Lord. Sickness can drive us to the reality that we are not going to live forever, and God's Word can help us think rightly about that realization.

In fact, James goes on to say in verse 15, "Instead, you ought to say, 'If the Lord wills, we shall live and also do this or that.'" Our lives are brief, and they are not under our control. God is in control of our lives. We may think we know how our lives are going to turn out, but God is the only One who knows and controls. No Christian, or anyone else, can safely assume that he can live independently of God.[19] It is arrogant to assume our lives will go just as we plan. Sickness can shock us out of that foolish speculation into reality.

Life is short, sickness can linger, and death is sure, but God is eternally sovereign over all of it. Death claims 100 percent of its victims, and all suffer sickness along the way; some suddenly, some gradually, but all will suffer it. It is in the midst of that sickness that we can become much more aware of our momentary lives. Suffering through sickness in a godly manner can open our eyes to our mortality and fragility, and that is a good thing. We are in effect being taught how to rightly value our days in light of life's brevity.

---

18 J. Strong, *A Concise Dictionary of the Words in the Greek Testament and the Hebrew Bible* (Bellingham, WA: Logos Bible Software), 1:17.
19 F. E. Gaebelein et al., eds., *The Expositor's Bible Commentary: Hebrews through Revelation* (Grand Rapids: Zondervan, 1981), 12:197.

Scripture tells us to value the days given us by God (Ps. 90:12). That command alone is sufficient for us to live realistically, not in speculation. Yet with some people, the Lord sees fit to extend His textbook lesson to everyday life. Some not only get to read about why and how they should value their God-given mortality, they get to participate in the lab of life that reinforces the all-sufficient textbook of Scripture. Walking with the Lord through long-term sickness or injury will change the way we value the God-given gift of life. It will also change the way we value God, who has given us life. As a result, it can encourage us to glorify Him by serving Him with whatever time and energy He has allotted us.

God's use of sickness in our lives can open our eyes to how fragile we are and how brief our life is. When understood biblically, sickness will direct our thoughts back to our sovereign God, help us to value what He has given us, and motivate us, even in a fragile state, to serve Him the best we can with what we have. The restricting of a believer's life should cause him or her to value what life is left and to use it to better glorify God qualitatively if not quantitatively. Our life is short. We ought to trust the Lord and serve Him with what is left. This is the third benefit of sickness; it teaches us to think more biblically, more realistically, about our life and God.

Hope

Sickness can lead us into much hope. Sickness can be an aid in helping us discern our heart by revealing what is inside, whether good or bad. This happens much like how a winepress reveals what is inside a grape as it squeezes and presses the grape. When a grape is squeezed, that which is inside comes out. When the Lord uses divinely designed circumstances, like long-term sickness or injury, to squeeze and press us, that which is inside will come out. It is through that squeezing process and because of that squeezing process that the fourth benefit of sickness can be realized. The squeezing process is the God-ordained start to a hope-filled chain of events in our life. So, the fourth way sickness can be beneficial is that its pressing nature can lead us to real hope.

The apostle Paul knew all about being squeezed and pressed. Within the larger theme of the book of Romans, which is the justifying righteousness that comes from God unto the guilty sinner by grace alone through faith in Christ alone, Paul taught about the pressing nature of tribulations. These are tribulations that befall the believer due to his relationship with Christ. Furthermore, concerning these tribulations, Paul taught that the believer is not lost but, rather, tempered through tribulations by the empowering and indwelling Holy Spirit.

Paul taught that one's salvation is preserved not by human effort but because a believer is eternally bound to Jesus Christ by His salvific power. In Romans 4, it was Christ's work that saved the sinner by giving him the gift of faith and reckoning righteousness to him (4:3). Now, in chapter 5, it is Christ's work that keeps the sinner saved.

That being said, the section of Scripture with which we are dealing is not directly about sickness. It is about eternal security found in the Savior. However, there is a universal principle that is both relevant and can be applied to our context. In Romans 5:3–4 we see the universal principle we are after when Paul says, "And not only this, but we also exult in our tribulations, knowing that tribulation brings about perseverance; and perseverance, proven character; and proven character, hope."

The universal principle is that God sovereignly ordains our tribulations to bring about hope. Our tribulation is not random, and it is not outside God's control. No, our tribulation has a purpose behind it and has been ordained by our loving heavenly Father.

Looking back at verse 3, we see Paul starts out saying, "And not only this." Not only this, what? Paul is referring, in part, to the reality of verses 1 and 2. Not only do believers have a present, objective "peace with God through our Lord Jesus Christ" (v. 1), and not only do believers have a permanent standing with God—that is, a permanent access to God—by Jesus Christ (v. 2), Paul also knows there is a good purpose in our present tribulations. If God has granted us peace with Him and access to Him in verses 1 and 2, through the death of His Son in verses 6 through 8, then why wouldn't He have a good purpose behind our tribulation in verses 3 through 4?

So, not only do we have peace with God but we also have a permanent standing with God, and along with those truths we have a divine purpose in our tribulations. Clearly, at least two truths are implied in that statement. One, there will be tribulation in the believer's life. And two, God has a good purpose in that tribulation.

Seeing that tribulation is a reality and that God's divine hand is behind the tribulation, how are believers supposed to react? In verse 3 Paul says that "we also exult in our tribulations." The placement of the word translated as "also" is emphatic in the Greek sentence structure, which means that Paul is stressing it. The word *also*, used here, simply means "likewise" or "in addition to." So the construction in Greek would read "but also we exult." Paul is exulting over his objective peace and permanent standing with God, thanks to Christ, and likewise, he also exults in his tribulations.

We need to catch the idea here. In the same manner or along with his exulting over his peace and standing with God, which was all by the grace of God, he exults in his tribulation, which is ordained by God. Paul is saying he exults not only over God's graciousness to him realized through life with Christ and the peaceful standing that comes with that but also the suffering. Paul does not thank the Lord for some but rebel against the other. No, he exults in all of it in an equal manner.

Now, what exactly does Paul mean when he says "exult"? The Greek word used here for *exult* means to boast, to glory, to brag, to be proud of, or to rejoice. It gives the sense of displaying or proclaiming publicly and being satisfied with, in this case, another's achievements.

This verb is also in the present tense, and it is debated as to whether it is middle or passive in voice. The tense of the verb tells us that the exulting is a habitual practice. It is an always-practiced, present reality in Paul's life. The voice of the verb tells us in which way the subject realizes the action. If it is passive, it would mean that the subject is being acted upon. For example, in Mark 1:9, "Jesus . . . *was baptized* by John in the Jordan" (italics added).[20] Jesus, the subject, was receiving the action of baptizing. If it is middle voice it would mean that the subject is performing the action upon himself. For example, if we say, "I am *washing* myself," the "washing" is in the middle voice. We identify our verb as a passive-voice verb, but either way this is taken, God is still ultimately behind the action. So Paul is saying because of the peace given

---

20 Corey Keating, "Greek Verbs (Shorter Definitions)," Grammatical Voice of Verbs, accessed May 29, 2018, https://www.ntgreek.org/learn_nt_greek/verbs1.htm.

him by God (v. 1), and because of the permanent access to God (v. 2), and because of the divine purpose of tribulation in his life, because of God's working in, on, and through him, he keeps exulting in his tribulations.

Whereas in verse 2 Paul exulted in the hope of his promised glory to come, in verse 3 he also is exulting in the present tribulations. He is satisfied and content with what Christ has achieved for His people (providing peace with and access to God), and he is also satisfied with what Christ is achieving in him through his suffering. Paul is proud of the Lord using suffering in his life. He is rejoicing that through suffering he can display his love and loyalty to his Lord. And he is publicly proclaiming it. This is nothing new, and this is not isolated to Paul.

In Acts 5 Peter and the apostles had preached Christ crucified before the Sanhedrin. Most of the council wanted to kill them because of their message (v. 33). However, Gamaliel, the most noted rabbi of his time, advised against killing them (vv. 34–39). The council listened to him, yet they could not let the apostles get away with preaching another religion, so they had them severely flogged (v. 40).

What was the apostles' response? Verse 41 says, "So they went on their way from the presence of the Council, rejoicing that they had been considered worthy to suffer shame for His name." Believers rejoice when by their suffering they can show their love and loyalty to the Savior.[21] Is that how we respond to tribulation? We probably are not receiving a physical beating for Christ, but we do come under suffering. Do we complain our way through it? Do we become bitter

---

21 F. E. Gaebelein et al., eds., *The Expositor's Bible Commentary: Romans through Galatians* (Grand Rapids: Zondervan), 10:57.

when under suffering? Do we ask, "Why me?" We ought not respond like that. Instead, we ought to exult in God because we have been counted worthy to suffer in a way that produces sanctification as well as glory to God.

If Paul, Peter, and the other apostles are doing that, and if they expect their original audience to do that, are not we also expected to do that? Is this not how we are to respond to tribulation—in faith and submission to our Lord? Has not Christ also given us the same eternal gifts (peace with and access to God)? And with those eternal gifts, are there not also temporal tribulations? Yes! And we are to practice exulting in our Lord and how He is achieving His purposes in us.

Remember, our universal principle is that God sovereignly ordains our tribulations to bring about hope, as Paul has said in Romans 5:3-4: "And not only this, but we also exult in our tribulations, knowing that tribulation brings about perseverance; and perseverance, proven character; and proven character, hope." Now what is the Lord using to achieve His purpose of sanctification in us in Romans 5? He is achieving it in us in our tribulations (v. 3). The Greek word used here for "tribulations" means to press or crush from the outside. This is pressing, crushing tribulation from the outside brought on by one's relationship with Christ. Paul is also exulting in the pressing or crushing of tribulations in his life.

But why Paul? Why would he rejoice in that? Well, not only because of the truths in verses 1 and 2 but also because of the divinely designed chain in verses 3 and 4.

In the second half of verse 3, Paul says that he knows, understands, and recognizes something. He knows the truth of, understands the meaning about, and recognizes the progression through—as well as the ultimate outcome of—his tribulations. Paul gets it. Paul's circumstances may not have changed, but he gets it. Moreover, he values it. What? He values it? Is Paul some kind of masochist? No, he values the divine chain of suffering God has ordained for him because the journey will produce in him qualities that will be useful and glorifying to God.

How do we know this is the case? How do we know Paul recognizes and understands what is going on? Because Paul identifies the first and second links in this chain in the second half of verse 3 when he says, "Tribulation brings about perseverance." If someone can correctly observe, explain, and apply something, then obviously, they understand it. Paul is doing just that. He starts explaining that this tribulation is the first link, and the perseverance he has acquired is the second.

The Greek word for "perseverance," *hupomonē*, is often translated as "patience." It also carries with it a sense of endurance. It paints the picture of being able to press on and overcome opposition or obstacles. Paul is saying that he realizes his suffering, and likewise our suffering, will—not *might* but *will*—bring about a more developed endurance. Just as the practice of running successively longer distances can train our bodies for endurance, so can long or repeated occurrence of tribulations train our soul for endurance. And Paul values this benefit.

He goes on to identify the third link in the chain: proven character (v. 4). The term Paul uses for "proven character," *dokimē*, simply means "proof." Proven character is a qualitative proof of something. It is a tested or proven value. The idea here is of a metallurgist testing, or proving, the quality of the material with which he is working. The proving process required much heat to burn off the dross—the worthless material—so as to arrive at the end product of a pure substance.

In our case, how can we take this? Surely, we don't need intense heat to burn off our dross, do we? Well, maybe we actually do. What was the heat source Paul was referring to? Paul was referring to God-ordained pressures of a nature and duration that required perseverance and patience. That was the heat source: divinely ordained and designed pressures and tribulations.

Tribulation, when responded to biblically, brings about perseverance in God's people so that they grow in character through the empowering Holy Spirit. In this context God used intense, long-term persecution as the fire in His people's lives to bring about proof of their character, or proven character.

Since this is so, is it not reasonable that God might use pressing, hot tribulations in our lives, with sufficient duration, to bring about proven character? Are we so arrogant to think that only Paul's original audience needed some dross removed? Maybe we need divinely arranged circumstances to burn off some dross in our lives. Is it not possible that our loving heavenly Father knows exactly what is needed to remove our dross and bring forth the pure substance? Surely, He does! To this fact John MacArthur says, "When Christians experience tribulations that demand perseverance, that perseverance, in turn, produces in them proven spiritual character. Just as a metalsmith uses intense heat to melt silver and gold in order to cleanse them of physical impurities, so does God use tribulations to cleanse His children of spiritual impurities."[22]

---

22 John MacArthur, *New Testament Commentary: Romans 1–8* (Chicago: Moody Press, 1991), 282.

Believer, God has a purpose behind our tribulations. God uses pressing, crushing circumstances—and in our context, long-term sickness or injury—to, in part, grow our character. That's the nature of progressive sanctification. Christ has saved us and given us peace (v. 1), He gave us access to the Father and has destined believers to share in the Father's glory (v. 2), and with that He divinely ordains tribulations in our life (v. 3). He does that because we need to be progressively sanctified on our way to being perfectly sanctified in glory.

Christ has saved us, but we cannot remain like newborns. We need to grow. He's made us holy in our position; now we need to become what we have already been declared: holy. God has ordained that that process is realized as we progress through the suffering. We can also exult in that suffering because we know what God is doing in us and what He will ultimately do with us. When we endure tribulation God's way—that is, by exulting in it—we can know with certainty that we will realize greater perseverance and proven character. We will progress in our sanctification. We will be a living demonstration of the power of the gospel!

But that is not where the chain ends. There is another link. And Paul says that link is hope (v. 4). Hope is the last link in this chain which consummates a series of links beginning with suffering. The Greek word for "hope" here is not like our idea of hope. This is not saying he hopes upon a star for something or that he wishes something would happen. No, this word for hope gives the sense of a reasonable and confident expectation of a future event.

This is the ultimate end. This is what Paul most exults in. Paul confidently exults in the completion of the chain. He is talking about the fulfillment of his suffering, or the bringing to a state of perfection. Paul confidently trusts the Lord to rightly end the process He has started in him. Paul knows that suffering for Christ and suffering like Christ (in humility and submission before the Father) all point to an end of life like, and with, Christ. Paul has real hope in God's eternal purposes for him.

Just as in verses 1 and 2, where Paul has a real hope of being in glory with God because he had been granted peace and a permanent standing with God, so he also has hope because it has been granted him to suffer for God. Our present sufferings help us to share in future glory with God because they are transforming us into the image of Christ. God has ordained the process of progressive sanctification as well as the end results. When we die, the only things we can take with us are the spiritual qualities Christ has progressively formed in us through sanctification. To this fact E. F. Harrison says, "Approved Christian character finds its ultimate resting place in the presence of God, not in a grave. By the tutelage of suffering the Lord is fitting us for his eternal fellowship."[23]

God uses tribulation to help us progress in our sanctification with a view to the end, which is our glorification. That is when we will be perfectly sanctified with Christ, and that is what Paul is ultimately hoping in. Paul knows he has already been given peace and access to God (vv. 1–2). He also knows that true "hope does not disappoint" because he has been given God's engagement ring, the Holy Spirit (v. 5). Paul knows that God will fulfill His promises and that he will stand in glory with God. If verses 1, 2, and 5 are true and to be trusted, are not verses 3 and 4 the same? Similar to how a bride-to-be confidently goes through all the preparations leading up to the actual realization of the marriage, so Paul

---

[23] Gaebelein et al, eds., 10:57.

confidently endures tribulation knowing and expecting to one day realize access to God in its fullest measure because of what Christ has done and is doing through him.

While God does use persecution to produce His desired ends, He can also use long-term sickness or injury to do the same. Our Lord can use sickness as the hot pressure through which our dross is removed. In so doing, proven character and hope realized will be the result. Take courage! The progression through sickness and disease is hard, but our promised and sure hope will one day be realized when we are standing before God in glory. Until that day, are our hearts fixed on that real hope or in changing circumstances? The next time we are crushed by tribulation, the answer will be revealed. In this way our God-ordained sickness will progress us in our sanctification, and that is a link in the chain that inevitably leads to hope realized. This is why Paul was exulting. This is the fourth benefit of sickness: real, eternal hope. Let us fix our eyes on it.

Comfort

The fifth way sickness can be beneficial is that it can be used to comfort and encourage. A long-term sickness or injury, when viewed biblically, can bring much solace and reassurance both to us and others. God is sovereign over all sickness and injury, and He does not just use such afflictions for sanctifying purposes alone. He also comforts us in the midst of them and makes us a conduit of His comfort to others. We can see this wonderful truth in 2 Corinthians 1:3–4.

But first, let's set up some background. Paul's purpose in writing 2 Corinthians was to defend his apostolic authority and ministry from the attack on it originating from within the Corinthian church. There were false teachers infiltrating the congregation at Corinth. They were seeking to teach what amounted to doctrines of demons over and above Paul's true teaching. The false teachers' wicked strategy was to engage in character assassination against Paul so the congregation would discount him and follow their false teachings.

After hearing about these false teachers, Paul left Ephesus abruptly and went to Corinth to confront the problem head on. The confrontation was painful and unsuccessful according to Paul. The congregation did not defend Paul against the false teachers' accusations. In fact, someone there actually confronted Paul with the false accusations as ammunition (2:1–2).

Therefore, Paul left the church he founded and went back to Ephesus. Paul was hoping to spare the congregation from further reproof, and he was hoping that time would bring the congregation to their senses (1:23). He did not want another painful, sorrow-producing visit to Corinth (2:1). Paul was not just concerned for his own sorrow over the demonic influence in the church but for the sorrow and pain his confrontation caused those in the congregation. Nonetheless, Paul was also committed to the church's purity. So, from Ephesus he penned his second letter to the Corinthian church and sent it to them.

The letter Paul wrote to the Corinthians was a hard letter for him. He was torn up inside. Paul loved the body at Corinth. It was painful to watch them buckle under the false teaching. As Paul wrote his second letter to the Corinthian congregation, his heart was filled with sorrow. His eyes were filled with tears, he was in anguish, and he was under the weight of that affliction (2:4).

Paul did not waver in his faith. He already trusted God's sovereign calling in his life (1:1). He knew he had been given objective peace with God and was a recipient of His grace. He recognized that God was the source of all mercies in his life as well as to all other believers. Likewise, he knew God was the source of all comfort, and comfort was exactly what Paul needed and wanted to give to the Corinthians (v. 3). Paul had received comfort, and he wanted to give it to others because they needed it too.

As in our last point, this section of Scripture is not directly about sickness. It's about a divinely strengthened Paul strengthening the Corinthians with a message of comfort and deliverance in the midst of affliction and trials. Nonetheless, a universal principle can be gleaned from the text at hand: God comforts His children during affliction. God's merciful comfort comes with God-ordained affliction; this is designed to strengthen the believer's trust in Him so he or she will be prepared to strengthen others in their affliction. God's comfort to the afflicted believer is not to end with the afflicted believer. That believer is to go and likewise comfort another in their affliction.

This divine message of trust and comfort is meant to be shared with others. God is behind everything, from the source of affliction to the means of divine comfort—through the human agent and His Word—during the affliction. And so God, through Paul, sends a message of divine comfort to believers during their affliction.

Since it's true that God comforts His people during affliction, we need to understand the terms Paul uses. To that end, let's briefly examine what Paul says in 2 Corinthians 1:3: "Blessed be the God and Father of our Lord Jesus Christ, the

Father of mercies and God of all comfort." Why does Paul in this context call God "blessed"? It is because Paul is praising God for comforting and encouraging Him during his recent time of deadly affliction in Asia (vv. 8–10).[24] Paul is highlighting some attributes of God for which he now has a greater appreciation due to his personal need and God's divine response to that need.[25]

Paul gives us the two attributes for which he is praising God. First, he says he is praising God because God is the "Father of mercies." God is not a detached deity. God did create the world and then take His hands off His creation, and He's is not a stoic, uncompassionate God. Paul says that God is a God of deep awareness and sympathy to the sufferings of His children.[26] God is a God of much mercy. He has given the Lord Jesus Christ, the biggest mercy of all. He gave Paul His limitless compassion, His mercy, in Paul's time of affliction.

Along with God's mercy, Paul has received the full quantity or extent—the completeness—of God's comfort. God has given Paul His never-failing comfort. And He has given it because, as the text says, God is the "God of all comfort." The Greek word for *comfort* here means "encouragement." It gives the sense of consolation. This is the act of giving relief in affliction, and Paul was both receiving it and wanting to extend it to the congregation at Corinth.

---

24 This difficult time for Paul, to which no details are attached, happened after his writing of the first letter to the Corinthians and somewhere in Ephesus.
25 F. E. Gaebelein et al., eds., *The Expositor's Bible Commentary: Romans through Galatians* (Grand Rapids: Zondervan, 1976), 10:320.
26 This is not saying that God in His essence is changeable nor that He is controlled by His emotions (but He is also complex as His ways and thoughts are higher than ours—Isa. 55:8–9—and He is beyond our understanding). He is in complete control of His emotions while holding them all simultaneously in perfect harmony under the umbrella of His holiness. At the same time, He does care about His people.

Paul was mourning, he was distraught, and he was sorrowful due to the demonic influence in the church, but within Paul's affliction, God comforted him. Matthew 5:4 says, "Blessed are those who mourn, for they shall be comforted." Paul was living in the reality of God's promise to comfort when he penned this letter to the Corinthians. He had experienced God's comfort through a deadly situation in Asia, and he is confident that God will comfort him while dealing with the congregation at Corinth.

So, the question might arise of the nature of the comfort Paul was experiencing. To answer this question, we should observe three facts:

1. As said above, the word *comfort* means encouragement, consolation, and the act of giving relief in affliction.
2. Paul's heart was still suffering a great deal of affliction at the time of writing his letter to the Corinthians.
3. Paul wrote the letter and praised God though in the midst of his affliction.

If we were to put those three observations together, we can see the nature of God's comfort to Paul. This was a comfort that strengthened Paul through encouragement and consolation so he could continue on in useful service to the Lord. In other words, God mercifully comforted Paul by strengthening him in the affliction so he could endure it.

That is a key lesson to learn. When we are under long-term burdens, when our hearts are heavy, when our bodies are breaking, and when our minds, even though dull from disease, are racing, we are to seek God's merciful comfort. And if we respond in righteousness, like Paul, we will experience God's comfort.

How many times does God need to say something for it to be true? One time. Yet God has mentioned His comfort in our affliction ten times in five verses (2 Corinthians 1:3–7)! There is no question about it; God *will* comfort the afflicted believer. He is the "God of all comfort."

Yet, we are to remember that God's merciful comfort may not come in the form of changed circumstances. We very well may not get better. However, God has promised His people that in their mourning, "they shall be comforted" (Matt. 5:4). We will be comforted to endure the God-ordained affliction with God-ordained strength. Paul had learned that lesson, and he was praising God for the strength to carry on with his mission despite the continuing afflictions.

If we are suffering greatly, we must trust our great merciful Lord to fulfill His promise to us. He will comfort us in our affliction. Let us not fix our hope on the snake oil of changing circumstances that was never promised. Let us fix our hope on the promise our God has made to us. He will help us endure our affliction so we can carry on with a life lived for Him—a life of strengthening and encouragement that is even contagious. Our trusting endurance through much suffering is a witness and encouragement to those around us. To this truth, Paul states in 2 Corinthians 1:4, "[God] comforts us in all our affliction so that we may be able to comfort those who are in any affliction with the comfort with which we ourselves are comforted by God."

Paul says that God is not only a merciful comforter but also a purposeful comforter. We who have received God's strengthening comfort are to take that comfort to others in affliction. We may not be able to leave our bed, but we may be able to talk to someone on the phone or talk with visitors—even if only for a few moments. And a few moments are all we need to spread the comfort of God's trustworthiness to someone. Paul trusts God in the midst of his affliction, and that is comforting to him. Now he wants to share the truth of God's goodness, comfort, and trustworthiness with others.

So how could this apply to someone who is sick? Here is one example. When someone who is suffering from terminal cancer asks their visitors how they might pray for them, that is an unforgettable display of God's fulfilled promise to comfort. It says, despite the condition, despite our circumstances, that God is trustworthy. He has comforted even in a deadly scenario so we can now share that comfort with others.

We have been called and empowered to share the comfort with others that we have received from our Lord. Since when have the Lord's mercies ever been meant to be kept to oneself? We are to tell others of how He has encouraged us through our affliction. We are to use our infirmity as a tool to share God's goodness with others. The affliction of sickness can indeed be used to comfort and encourage. This is the fifth benefit of sickness. Our Lord will comfort us in our affliction so we can be a conduit of comfort to others and thus glorify Him.

Ministry

The last way sickness can be beneficial is that it can enhance and increase our ministry. The Greek word for *ministry* (*diakonía*) means "service" or "to serve." The range of meaning behind the word also includes the idea of a slave or servant.[27]

When we are faced with long-term sickness or injury, it is easy to fall into the trap of thinking that our usefulness in

---

27 D. N. Freedman, et al., eds., *Eerdmans Dictionary of the Bible* (Grand Rapids: Eerdmans, 2000), s.vv. "minister," "ministry."

ministry, our service, is over. And yet everybody has a ministry for which they are responsible. Ministry is not only for the man behind the pulpit each Sunday. All believers are to share the gospel and walk in righteousness before a watching world. That is ministry. That is serving the Lord. And serving the Lord is worshiping the Lord.

Everybody has a sphere of influence in life. It may be a single person such as a caretaker, or it may be an entire congregation of people. A multiplicity of examples could be found between those two extremes—our coworkers, people we know at the gym (if well enough to go), the mail carrier, the waste-removal employee, teammates, or Bible study groups. Our sphere of influence has been personally ordained by God Himself. He has orchestrated the scope of people in our lives with whom we can share the good news about Christ. It is within that sphere of influence that we minister.

When someone falls ill and that condition persists for a long period of time, it is critically important that the afflicted believer remember three truths so they might persist in ministry:

1. God's ordination—God has sovereignly ordained the intensity, frequency, and duration of our sickness.
2. God's intention—God intends for us to put Him on display to others.
3. God's determination—God determines the type of ministry in which we are to engage.

So let's examine those three divine purposes in our sickness so we will have hope and encouragement to persist in ministry. One, the Lord is in complete control over the nature, intensity, frequency, and duration of our infirmity. His hands are not tied by someone's sickness. Moreover, God owns our body. It is on loan from Him to us. He has bought it with a great price (1 Cor. 6:19–20), and He can do with it as He pleases. And what He pleases is always for our good and His glory (Rom. 8:28–30). Therefore, it is not for us to grumble, complain, or despair about our sickness. It is only for us to seek how we might glorify Christ during our sickness.

If God chooses to use the body He has loaned us to glorify Himself through some degree of sickness, we have nothing to complain about. He is simply using His property in a way that brings Him the most glory and us the most good—even if not realized this side of heaven. No right has been taken from us if we are sick. We do not have the right to good health. God has the right to our health. He has the right to use the body He loaned us in the way He sees fit. A good self-diagnostic question to ask is this: Do we view our body as ours or on loan from the Lord to be used for His purposes? Our reaction to sickness will tell us which one we really believe.

That leads us to the second important truth to remember: God's intention. God intends for us to put Him on display to others. Even in our diminished state, the Lord still intends for us to be a witness for Him. That is great news! How many people does this world discount and even dispose of simply because they have diminished or limited capacity? The Lord does not do that to His people. He still uses them to glorify Himself.

In fact, the Lord uses those who are weak to even more clearly display His grace. In 2 Corinthians 12:9–10 Paul speaks to this fact when he relays the Lord's message to him after praying for relief from a tremendous affliction. Paul said, "And He has said to me, 'My grace is sufficient for you, for power is perfected in weakness.' Most gladly, therefore,

I will rather boast about my weaknesses, that the power of Christ may dwell in me. Therefore I am well content with weaknesses, with insults, with distresses, with persecutions, with difficulties, for Christ's sake; for when I am weak, then I am strong." This context is about great affliction against Paul in his ministry. The Lord, as the ultimate cause, used Satan, the immediate cause, and had ordained a satanically motivated and empowered false teacher to be a thorn in Paul's side.[28]

The purpose of this affliction against Paul was that of humility (2 Cor. 12:7). Prior to this event Paul had been given a tremendous vision of heaven by the Lord (vv. 1–4). Paul was aware of the potential for pride in his own life, and he wished to avoid that possibility (vv. 5–6). Obviously, the Lord knew the temptation for Paul and protected him from that outcome with the satanically inspired opposition. So while the context is not about sickness, the universal principle remains: even in the midst of affliction and weakness, the Lord can use us as a witness to His grace. We can still be a gospel witness amid our sickness. We do not need to, nor should we, just give up on ministering.

Paul asked the Lord to remove his affliction three times, but the Lord would not. Instead, and even better, the Lord

---

[28] We are taking the stance that this affliction was a demonically inspired false teacher for four reasons. One, the context of chapters 10–13 is about Paul fighting enemies (i.e., the false apostles). Two, the Greek word Paul uses (*angelos*), translated as "messenger" (12:7), speaks to an angel from Satan and not a physical illness. Third, the Greek word (*kolaphizō*), translated as "buffet" (v. 7), always speaks of wrongful treatment from another person (Matt. 26:67; Mark 14:65; 1 Cor. 4:11; 1 Peter 2:20). Fourth, the Old Testament describes Israel's physical opponents as thorns, just as Paul described his opponents in 12:7 (Num. 33:55; Josh. 23:13; Judg. 2:3; Ezek. 28:24). Thus, it seems very reasonable, considering the weight of evidence, to see Paul's affliction, the thorn in his side, as a demonically indwelled false teacher.

supplied continuing grace for Paul to endure the affliction. Now why was it better for the Lord to supply His continuous grace rather than removing the affliction? It was because as Paul endured in and pressed through the affliction, the power of Christ in him would be made manifest. Paul's crushing affliction remained, but Paul kept pressing on because God's grace in Paul's life kept on flowing.

The more blows that came Paul's way, the more he pressed on, the more God's glory shined through him. Therefore, Paul says that he is "well content with weaknesses, with insults, with distresses, with persecutions, with difficulties, for Christ's sake" (v. 10). It wasn't the pain that Paul took pleasure in. It was the power of Christ revealed in him through his responses to the affliction that he took pleasure in. And that degree of power would not have been as evident had God removed the affliction.

Paul did what we often do during our time of affliction. He asked the Lord to remove it. The Lord would not. Therefore, instead of focusing on the circumstances, which is what we also often do, he focused on the Lord. He focused on the Lord's graciousness and trusted Him to empower him to glorify Christ regardless of the circumstances. Paul counted the Lord and His glory as more important than his own relief. We ought to ask ourselves if we do that. Do we trust the Lord so much as to value His glory over and above our getting better?

Paul's correct view of the remedy to his affliction enhanced and increased his ministry. Because of Paul's trust in God's plan for him, he not only impacted the congregation at Corinth, he is impacting us two thousand years later. That is a long ministry lifespan!

What kind of impact might we have on people during our affliction? How might we shine forth the Lord's glory in our unrelieved state? When others know we are suffering, yet we offer to pray for them, that makes an impact for God's glory. When we are under pain and exhaustion but do not complain or expect another's world to revolve around us and instead offer to help them in some way, that shines forth God's glory. When visitors come to see us, observe our suffering, then begin to be troubled for us, yet we comfort them, that has an impact for God's glory. That displays the glory of Christ in our lives. Our ministry has just increased. Then we will see that we are "well content" with our weakness because it is in that weakness we have been made strong, and God is glorified through that strength.

Lastly, God determines the type of ministry in which we are to engage. Many of us have preconceived notions of how our ministry might pan out. We may have envisioned ourselves as a pastor of a church, a leader in women's ministries, a missionary overseas, or a housewife and homemaker. Or maybe we thought we would be a scholar in Bible translation. Whatever shape our idea of ministry may have taken, it is obvious after a prolonged sickness that things are not turning out how we envisioned they would.

We know that sickness is a blessing, it is for our benefit, it glorifies God, and we can still be useful. Nevertheless, we can struggle with the way in which we are being used. The core issue of the struggle comes down to trust. Reading Scripture and even others' writings about the topic can help us to trust that God will still use us. At the same time, we must also trust Him in how He uses us.

We must trust the Lord even if His vision of ministry is different from ours. After all, it is still for our good and His glory (Rom. 8:28–30). We cannot let our ideas, as good as they may have been, be the standard for the ministerial norm in our lives. We must submit to what God determines as the ministerial norm. We must submit to a new normal in our lives if the Lord calls us to it. More than that, we must even rejoice in that new normal. For an example of this, we again look to the apostle Paul. In Philippians 1:12–18 Paul says,

> Now I want you to know, brethren, that my circumstances have turned out for the greater progress of the gospel, so that my imprisonment in the cause of Christ has become well known throughout the whole praetorian guard and to everyone else, and that most of the brethren, trusting in the Lord because of my imprisonment, have far more courage to speak the word of God without fear. Some, to be sure, are preaching Christ even from envy and strife, but some also from good will; the latter do it out of love, knowing that I am appointed for the defense of the gospel; the former proclaim Christ out of selfish ambition, rather than from pure motives, thinking to cause me distress in my imprisonment. What then? Only that in every way, whether in pretense or in truth, Christ is proclaimed; and in this I rejoice.

Let's observe some truths about Paul's ministry and circumstances. At this time in Paul's life, he was imprisoned in Rome (ca. AD 61). All through his ministry, Paul had prayed and planned his way to Rome. He wanted to testify concerning the truth about Christ to the emperor himself. The type of ministry in which Paul planned to engage was an outreach to the power in Rome for the gospel.

Paul's idea of the ministerial norm was well established in his mind. He had planned how he would achieve and engage with his desired audience in Rome. However, God had a different idea of how Paul's ministry would look. In God's plan, Paul would still go to Rome; that part remained the same. But the way in which Paul got to Rome would be much different than he had imagined. Instead of Paul making his way to Rome as a preacher, he was taken to Rome as a prisoner. Paul's engagement in the ministry was much different than he had envisioned. Yet Paul was not downtrodden about the change. On the contrary, he embraced the new normal in his life.

He told the Philippians that his God-ordained chains, his imprisonment, and his circumstances actually "turned out for the greater progress of the gospel" (v. 12). Paul saw that through his imprisonment, he had an opportunity to reach people whom he may have never met otherwise. Paul didn't view his imprisonment as a hindrance to his ministry; he viewed it as an enhancement. In fact, it was such an enhancement that Paul got to preach to the emperor's guards and "to everyone else" there too (v. 13). Furthermore, Paul realized that his God-ordained new normal would serve to encourage others in their ministry. Even if other believers were threatened with arrest for sharing the gospel, they could remember Paul's example. Paul was arrested and now had a prison ministry of sorts. Others could do the same. Being arrested for sharing the gospel doesn't stop the spread of it. It simply gives one a new audience.

We might ask how this could apply to us. How could someone who is a shut-in due to sickness have an enhanced ministry? Well, even shut-ins must go for doctors' visits. Even shut-ins have trips to the emergency room.

Think of the people at the doctor's office or in hospitals. Without that trip to the doctor or hospital, which we are so quick to judge as bad, we may have never met the people there. We may have never had the opportunity to share the gospel with nurses, doctors, or other patients. How about the ambulance drivers that came to pick us up? When might we have met them if not for sickness? They need Christ too.

We may not be able to say much in our time of need, but we may be able to say something. We can at least suffer in a way that pleases and glorifies Christ. We do not have to suffer like the world suffers. When trials like physical pain press in on them, that which comes out of them is usually profanity because their heart is wicked (see Matt. 15:17–18). They are their own standard.

What about a believer? We have a much different standard. We have Christ. It would be beneficial to ask how He endured physical and emotional trauma. How did Christ suffer? While He suffered, He uttered no threats. While being reviled during His suffering, He did not revile in return but entrusted Himself to the Father (1 Peter 2:22–24). If there was ever a time that Christ might have some kind of sinful response to His circumstances, it would have been during His crucifixion. Yet He had no such response. Instead, He trusted the Father. How then should we suffer? Even if we cannot say much, we can suffer well before a watching world. We can demonstrate that we trust the Lord even in the direst of circumstances. That was what Paul was demonstrating as well, in word and deed.

Paul says that even while ministering under arrest he had critics. He said that some were "preaching Christ even from envy and strife" (Phil. 1:15). Some of Paul's contemporaries were preaching Christ but preaching Christ with a desire of self-advancement. They knew Paul was under arrest, so they wanted to take his place in preaching. They were in contention with Paul, and that was seen in their strife against him. Paul's critics had discredited him, and this group of self-centered preachers were jumping all over the opportunity to grab the limelight in Paul's absence.

In fact, they were even proclaiming that Paul was imprisoned due to some kind of sin.[29] They were preaching Christ with wrong motives: they were preaching Christ from envy, they resented Paul's gifting and saw him as a threat to their own authority and strife, and they wanted to fight against Paul (v. 15). Paul says that these men were doing what they were doing "out of selfish ambition, . . . thinking to cause me distress in my imprisonment" (v. 17). They wanted to discredit Paul, and what better way than to attack his character by claiming he was in prison because of sin rather than gospel progress (vv. 12–13). This was painful and discouraging to Paul's heart, not because of his reputation but because of the danger it posed to the church's purity.

At the same time, not everyone preaching Christ in Paul's absence was doing it with wrong motives. Paul said there were some who sought to stand in the gap and keep proclaiming the same message out of love for Paul and the Lord. He said that some preach "out of love, knowing that I am appointed for the defense of the gospel" (v. 16).

Nonetheless, whether the gospel was preached with wrong or right motives, it was being preached. Either way, the truth was being heard, and in those circumstances, Paul rejoiced.

Now, someone might ask how Paul could express joy in those situations. He could exult in a ministry that was much

---

[29] John F. MacArthur Jr., *Philippians Commentary* (Chicago: Moody, 2001), 63–65.

different than what he had envisioned because he firmly trusted in God's sovereignty. Paul trusted in the new normal that the Lord had ordained for his life. Paul trusted that neither chains nor others' bad motives would hinder the gospel. Paul knew that God's gospel was not contingent on his circumstances. Paul was not foremost concerned about fulfilling *his* vision of ministry. He was primarily concerned with ministering in the way God had ordained for him to fulfill.

How about us? Are we more wrapped up in ministering the way we think we ought to minister or in ministering the way God says we are to minister? We need to examine our own heart. What is our response when we cannot engage in ministry the way we wanted? Is there anger in our heart? Is our knee-jerk reaction "Why me?" instead of "Why not me?" Do we ask, "Why this?" instead of "How might this be used?" Is sickness seen as a hindrance to our ministry instead of a help?

When circumstances are contrary and even if people are wrongly condemning us for our infirmities, do we rejoice with Paul that the gospel will still go out? Do we trust that the Lord's new normal for us is better than the plans we had? We ought to take the time to proclaim our joy along with Paul. And, like Paul, it should be a joy that the gospel will still advance and that the Lord will still use us even if He chooses to confine us to a bed, much as He did Paul to a guard.

This is the sixth benefit of sickness. The Lord can use affliction in the form of sickness to enhance and even create ministry opportunities for us in order to display His grace through us.

Conclusion

How wonderful, gracious, and merciful is our Lord to include so many benefits along with our ordained sickness. Our sickness is not out of His control, it is not random, and it is not purposeless. Our loving Lord uses sickness in our lives for good. He uses sickness to progressively sanctify and conform us to His image. During that conforming process we can take courage because He has promised to help us glorify Him. He has promised to conform us more to Christ's image. He helps us think more realistically. He provides real hope and comforts us. We can use all those benefits to minister to other believers as well as to be a witness to the unbelieving, watching world. The fact that our great God purposes and uses sickness in His people's lives ought to be a huge encouragement to us. It means our Lord is thinking about us. His attention is on us, and His intention is to purify us for our good and His glory. That is something we can praise Him for even in the midst of our suffering.

Bibliography

Adams, Jay, E. *The Christian Counselor's Manual: The Practice of Nouthetic Counseling.* Grand Rapids: Zondervan, 1973.

———. *What to Do on Thursday: A Layman's Guide to the Practical Use of the Scriptures.* Rev. Ed. Woodruff, SC: Timeless Texts, 1995.

Beckford, James A. *Cult Controversies: The Societal Response to New Religious Movements.* New York: Tavistock, 1985.

Cross, Frank Leslie, and Elizabeth A. Livingstone, eds. *The Oxford Dictionary of the Christian Church.* 3rd rev. ed. Oxford; New York: Oxford University Press, 2005.

Feinberg, John, S. *No One Like Him: The Doctrine of God.* Wheaton, IL: Crossway, 2001.

Geisler, Norman L. and William E. Nix. *From God to Us: How We Got Our Bible.* Chicago: Moody Publishers, 1974.

———. *A General Introduction to the Bible.* Rev. and expanded. Logos Bible Software. Chicago: Moody Press, 1986.

Grenz, Stanley J., David Guretzki, and Cherith Fee Nordling. *Pocket Dictionary of Theological Terms.* Downers Grove, IL: InterVarsity, 1999.

Grudem, Wayne A. *Systematic Theology: An Introduction to Biblical Doctrine.* Grand Rapids: Inter-Varsity Press; Zondervan, 2004.

Henry, Carl Ferdinand Howard. *God, Revelation, and Authority*. Wheaton, IL: Crossway, 1999.

Long, Jason. *Biblical Nonsense: A Review of the Bible for Doubting Christians*. Lincoln, NE: iUniverse, 2005.

MacArthur, John, ed. *The MacArthur Study Bible*. Nashville: Word Pub., 1997.

———. *The MacArthur Topical Bible: A Comprehensive Guide to Every Major Topic Found in the Bible*. Nashville: Thomas Nelson, 2010.

MacArthur, John. *Unleashing God's Word in Your Life*. Nashville: Thomas Nelson, 2003.

MacArthur, John F., Jr, Wayne A. Mack, and Master's College. *Introduction to Biblical Counseling: Basic Guide to the Principles and Practice of Counseling*. Dallas: Word Pub., 1997.

Mack, Wayne, A. "The Sufficiency of Scripture in Counseling." *The Master's Seminary Journal* 9, no.1 (Spring 1998). Accessed November 16, 2012. http://www.tms.edu/tmsj/tmsj9d.pdf.

Packer, J. I. *Concise Theology: A Guide to Historic Christian Beliefs*. Wheaton, IL: Tyndale House, 1993.

Smith, Robert D. MD, *The Christian Counselor's Medical Desk Reference*. Stanley, NC: Timeless Texts, 2000.

Snider, Andrew. "Theology 1 Content Syllabus." F12a Fall 2012. Sun Valley, CA: Grace Books International, 2012.

Street, John. "God's Agenda For Trouble." NANC.org. Accessed November 7, 2012. http://www.nanc.org/Resources/NANC-Library/General-Counseling/General-Cousenling-Documents/71trouble--street.aspx .

VanGemeren, Willem A., ed. *New International Dictionary of Old Testament Theology and Exegesis*. Grand Rapids: Zondervan, 1997.

Ware, Bruce A. *God's Greater Glory: The Exalted God of Scripture and the Christian Faith*. Wheaton, IL: Crossway, 2004.

On Campus & Distance Options Available

GRACE BIBLE THEOLOGICAL SEMINARY

Interested in becoming a student or supporting our ministry?
Please visit gbtseminary.org